*f*P

BOUNCE BACK

OVERCOMING SETBACKS TO SUCCEED IN BUSINESS AND IN LIFE

BY JOHN CALIPARI

with David Scott

Free Press

New York London Toronto Sydney

Free Press
A Division of Simon & Schuster, Inc.
1230 Avenue of the Americas
New York, NY 10020

Copyright © 2009 by John Calipari and David Scott

All rights reserved, including the right to reproduce this book or portions thereof in any form whatsoever. For information address Free Press Subsidiary Rights Department, 1230 Avenue of the Americas, New York, NY 10020.

First Free Press hardcover edition September 2009

FREE PRESS and colophon are trademarks of Simon & Schuster, Inc.

For information about special discounts for bulk purchases, please contact Simon & Schuster Special Sales at 1-866-506-1949 or business@simonandschuster.com.

The Simon & Schuster Speakers Bureau can bring authors to your live event. For more information or to book an event contact the Simon & Schuster Speakers Bureau at 1-866-248-3049 or visit our website at www.simonspeakers.com.

Designed by Julie Schroeder

Manufactured in the United States of America

3   5   7   9   10   8   6   4

Library of Congress Cataloging-in-Publication Data
Calipari, John.
Bounce back : overcoming setbacks to succeed in business and in life /
John Calipari and David Scott.
p. cm.
1. Success—Psychological aspects.   2. Self-management (Psychology)
I. Scott, David. II. Title.
BF637.S8C276 2009
155.2'4—dc22   2009022824

ISBN: 978-1-4165-9750-6
ISBN: 978-1-4165-5946-7 (ebook)

Excerpt from *The Bounce Back Book* by Karen Salmansohn. Copyright © 2007 by Karen Salmansohn. Used by permission of Workman Publishing Co., Inc., New York. All rights reserved.

Reprinted with the permission of Fireside, a division of Simon & Schuster, Inc., from *The Rhythm of Life: Living Every Day with Passion and Purpose*, New Edition by Matthew Kelly. Copyright © 1999 by Matthew Kelly. Revised edition copyright © 2005 by Beacon Publishing.

Excerpt from *The Success Principles* by Jack Canfield. Copyright © 2005 by Jack Canfield. Used by permission from HarperCollins.

For: Ellen, Erin, Megan, and Bradley—there are no bounce backs without the support and security of my amazing family.

CONTENTS

CONTENTS

**A portion of the proceeds from sales of *Bounce Back* will go to
the Calipari Family Foundation for Children. For more information
on the charity, please visit: www.coachcal.com.**

INTRODUCTION

Letter from Cal

Every summer—after I've had time to digest the previous season—I send a letter to all my players. In it I put forth my expectations for the season and set the tone for what we will work to accomplish when we begin play in November. For you, the reader, the following is your introductory letter to becoming a member of my Bounce Back Team.

February 2009

Dear Bounce-Back Team Member:

Who would have ever guessed something good would come from blowing a nine-point lead with two minutes and twelve seconds to go in the 2008 NCAA men's basketball championship game?

But the loss of my former team, the Memphis Tigers, in that game, the devastation of that bitter end to the 2007–08 season and the way we all dealt with the aftermath provided the impetus for me to write this book, which I envision helping you get through your own personal bounce back. A lot has changed since those two minutes and twelve seconds transpired. There's been another fantastic season of college basketball played; a new and worthy champion, the University of North Carolina, won the 2009 national title; and I've left the University of Memphis for the dream job I accepted at the University of

Kentucky on April 1, 2009. But the experiences, lessons, and results of that magical 2007–08 campaign will live forever with me, and now, hopefully with you. That's the silver lining I've discovered—knowing that the total, public humiliation of letting that lead slip away will now help me to touch lives in a positive way that otherwise would not have been possible.

Simply by reading and embracing the messages within this book, you will become a member of a special team—*my* team. The circumstances that led you to pick up this book—separation, divorce, foreclosure, downsizing, firing—have no bearing on how you came to the team. The important thing is, you found it, and you are willing to let me coach you through this period in your life. You have already taken a huge first step by acknowledging you need some guidance and direction.

You are part of a diverse group of people, and that diversity is something I'm quite comfortable with. My team at Kentucky (and before that at the University of Memphis and the University of Massachusetts) has always had players from diverse backgrounds and social levels. They come to me from various sets of life experiences. Some have been from privileged backgrounds, others were from middle-class homes, but most have been underprivileged African American adolescents whose young lives have been characterized by one bounce back after another. I'm proud to say I've been able to impact on their lives in positive ways, and I will do the same for you now that you're part of my team. Some of my guys have gone to the NBA, like Marcus Camby, Derrick Rose, and Tyreke Evans, but the majority of my former players have gone on to the "real world" far away from the arenas, the gyms, and the adulation. It is their stories of success and the overcoming of odds that I share most often. Nothing is more gratifying to me than having former players come back and thank me for the tough love and the coaching I provide for each and every young man.

Hopefully my impact on you will have a similar resonance. Everyone reading this book is coming to it from a different place. Some are incredibly wealthy, some are incredibly poor. Some have been knocked down before, and some are "rookies" entering their very first bounce-back experience. I've had two significant—public—bounce backs in my first fifty years of life, and I fully expect there to be others. Almost no one goes through life unscathed, and the ability to overcome obstacles is often what separates the haves from the have-nots.

The pages that follow will be your personal playbook to overcoming whichever of life's obstacles have brought you here. This is a book about coaching you through your bounce back, and when basketball experiences serve as illustrations for your benefit, I've included them. There are all sorts of setbacks in life; they can be as varied as the people who are affected by them. You are not the first to be dealing with the emotions and strife that result from life's obstacles, and you will not be the last. But by the time we are finished, you will be in a better position mentally and emotionally, I promise you that.

Whatever it is that has spurred you to pick up this book, there are certain undeniable rungs on the ladder of a bounce back that everyone will deal with. It's your ability to face the challenges head-on and with a positive mental attitude that will determine the ultimate success of your revitalization. Don't be fearful of the odd sensations that accompany the climb up the ladder; they are perfectly normal. Without them, you wouldn't be human.

Let me be the first to tell you, in brutally honest terms, that this could very well be one of the toughest undertakings you've faced in your life. There will be days when you think you have taken two steps up the ladder only to find out you have actually taken two steps down. You may feel depressed, defeated, or dispirited. At times it may seem like there is no hope and you are living in a permanent state of darkness. But I'm here to tell you those feelings will not last forever. You just need to work through them and allow me to coach you. Put your faith in me, and I will do the same with you.

The only one who can turn your situation around is *you*. That doesn't mean you can't solicit and accept help, but it does mean you are the main character in the story we are about to write of your bounce back. In fact, you will be doing a fair share of writing throughout this book, so be aware that you cannot be passive in any way, shape, or form. My Kentucky team works past exhaustion, and for your bounce back you will need to do the same.

You are going to be active with our whole team of bounce backers who are already congregating at a website I have set up: **www .coachcalbounceback.com.** At that site, we are building a community of bounce-back team members who will share their ups, their downs, their triumphs, and their tips. Think of it as our Players' Lounge, where we can congregate, commiserate, and coalesce as a unit. I encourage you to visit the site often and take part in the discussions and the sharing we are doing.

In 1999 when I was fired by the NBA's New Jersey Nets in a very public manner, I needed what you now hold in your hands—a book which would let me know that what I was going through was perfectly normal and all part of a multistage process that would eventually lead to my bounce-back job (for me it meant returning to the college game at Memphis, where we went to two Elite 8s and a Final Four). For you it can mean a new career, a new significant other, or a fresh start altogether.

Because of the many facets to a bounce back, this book is meant to be digested in bites. You are welcome to pop in and out as your own personal bounce back unfolds. Some of you may be well into your job search, and others may still be "under the covers." But what's more important is that you recognize that you're not alone. Millions of people are going through life's turmoil, and every one of them has a lesson to be shared, a tip to offer, or a word of hope that will inspire you.

Your teammates and I are here for you. Lean on us, and form a trust and bond so when you're able, you can turn around and help the next person on the ladder behind you. Your goal is to help yourself first, then at some point down the road, you will help others. It may seem unimaginable now, but soon you will be the one *giving* guidance, not receiving it.

You have to be willing to put in the time and be willing to be persistent with your bounce back, and you need to be coachable. Listen to my words and those of the experts I've reached out to—because we have been there before. The best way to learn is by having the advice of those who have been in your place before.

As I told my eventual Final Four, national runner-up Memphis team in their August 2007 letter prior to the 2007–08 season, "Let's all work with perfection in mind as we work on our weak areas. To talk in these terms may put more pressure on us, but in my opinion the only pressure is to prepare this summer like it's your last summer to prepare—the rest will take care of itself. If we do prepare with a passion for perfection, we will all expect to win every game whoever the opponent. To reach your personal goals, we must be playing on the last day!"

I'm not naive enough to think my letter was the reason our Memphis team won more college basketball games than any team ever had in a single season (thirty -eight) and had winning streaks of twenty-six and twelve games, or why we became a true, once-in-a-generation "dream team," but I do know my one-page, preseason letter put everyone in the same mind-set as we strove toward our goal.

That's what this letter is meant to do for you.

What I discuss within this book are many of the same principles I discuss when Fortune 500 companies ask me to come and coach their workforces. Bounce backs are constantly cropping up in the business world—especially now—and there are many parallels between what I do with my Kentucky team and what international corporations should be doing with their employees and resources. Business—and life—is all about bouncing back. **It's not about how far you fall but how high you rebound.**

In fact, in the time since I began working on this book, I have encountered an array of people and stories of famous (and not-so-famous) folks who have gone through their own bounce backs. Some were fired from their jobs, others were laid off, and many had seen their retirement funds shrink substantially or their homes face foreclosure, and still more were enduring a separation from a loved one.

Together, we will get you through whatever it is you are attacking right now. Stay with me and don't cheat yourself in any way. Let me coach you through your bounce back. I will coach you until that point in time when you are ready to coach yourself and then others. I am looking forward to this journey with you and all the challenges it will present. My teams always get better over the course of a season, and, likewise, you will improve over the duration of this book.

Are you ready? Let's get started . . .

Your Coach,

Coach Cal

SECTION I

. . .

IT'S ABOUT YOU

CHAPTER 1

THE TRIGGER EVENT

COMING TO GRIPS
WITH WHAT HAS HAPPENED

Numb.

I was just numb all over. In the span of about half an hour I went from near ecstasy to near anguish. *The confetti was falling for the wrong team*, I thought. *That should be us out there celebrating a national title.* Instead, we were taking a long short-walk to our locker room. "Man, that should have been us," I said to no one in particular.

On a muggy night in San Antonio on the first Monday of April 2008, my former team—the University of Memphis Tigers—was on the cusp of winning the NCAA title game over the University of Kansas. Our team had lost just once in thirty-nine prior games that season (to Tennessee by four points). We had won more single-season games than any program in NCAA history, and with two minutes and twelve seconds left in the national championship contest, we led the Jayhawks by nine points, 60–51.

With 2:12 showing on the scoreboard, the cavernous Alamodome was filled with 43,257 blue-and-white–clad fans (the colors of both teams), but it was our Tiger supporters who were scream-ing loudest and enjoying the moment the most. Yes, they were celebrating—and they should have been. The game was all but over.

When you're up nine with just over two minutes to go, you're supposed to win the game. It's that simple. Our best player—and the eventual No. 1 overall pick in the 2008 NBA draft and the 2008–09 NBA Rookie of the Year—Derrick Rose was having one of the great second halves in Final Four history on his way to eighteen points and eight assists. We had Kansas, one of the most storied basketball pro-grams of all time, on the ropes, and we probably only needed one more basket to knock them out.

Now understand this: Memphis hadn't ever won a national championship in *anything*. It was just the third Final Four appear-ance in Memphis school history (Kansas was making its thirteenth trip), and to be honest, our program wasn't perceived as a "Fortune 500" operation the way schools like Duke, UCLA, Kentucky, and North Carolina are. Memphis wasn't supposed to crash this party in San Antonio. But ever since I'd arrived in the Bluff City, I'd built the program as if we were one of the blue bloods. In everything we did, from recruiting to travelling, I instilled the belief that we were a pre-mier program on a par with any in the country. We recruited (and got) McDonald's All-Americans, and we fostered future pros. I never accepted that "people" didn't think of Memphis that way, and I never allowed my teams to think that way. My teams will always "strive for perfection and settle for excellence." I hope you'll adopt that mantra in your own bounce back.

We deserved just as much respect and rankings as anyone, so long as we were putting in our maximum effort. Pedigree is of little importance to me; it's what you do game to game and season to sea-son that determines what kind of program you will be.

We had been doing those things consistently for over half the decade. In 2008 we advanced to our third straight Elite 8 and finally busted through to the final weekend and the final game.

Our 2007–08 Tiger team embraced my "anyone, anywhere, any-time" philosophy, and with three NBA draft picks among my starting five (Rose, Chris Douglas-Roberts, and Joey Dorsey), we had unparalleled leadership and a supporting cast that combined experience with exceptional talent. We had been to those two consecutive Elite 8s with our core group, and the 2007–08 campaign was the culmination of an unprecedented run of 104 wins and just 10 losses in three seasons.

It brought us to that Monday night of April 7, 2008, before an international TV audience and an arena filled with luminaries, from Jesse Jackson (who spoke to our team prior to the game) to Bill Russell.

With two minutes and twelve seconds left, there would have to be a perfect storm of misfortune for us to lose the game.

We didn't know it at the time, but the seas were churning as Kansas scored on its next possession to cut the lead to seven with 1:57 left. Their coach and my friend, Bill Self, called a time-out, and when we inbounded the ball after the time-out, it got stolen, and Kansas hit a 3-pointer to cut the lead to four. A few seconds later, Joey, my center, who had been hampered by fouls throughout, finally fouled out.

Right about then, it struck me we might lose the game. Oddly, I reconciled those thoughts by quickly telling myself that if we were to lose, it would be because it was part of a bigger design. *Lord,* I said to myself, *I will deal with the outcome and your will.* That helped to force those losing thoughts out of my mind. But it didn't help to alter what was happening on the court. Kansas was doing everything right, and we were doing just about everything wrong.

With a minute left in the game, our lead was just two points. We missed three of our last four free throws in regulation, and Kansas's Mario Chalmers hit a miracle 3-pointer to send the game into overtime after a desperation shot from midcourt in the final seconds by my forward Robert Dozier missed. I knew we were in trouble in the extra session because my guys were gassed, we were stunned, and we didn't have Joey to rebound the ball. The perfect storm had happened, and it came at us with a fury as sudden as it was devastating.

Everything that had to go wrong for us to lose like we did happened. We had a late foul on Mario Chalmers, he had to make two free throws, and he did. Kansas's Darrell Arthur had to make an unbelievable turnaround jumper on the baseline. We threw away the ball on the inbounds pass. Sherron Collins stole it and made a 3-pointer. We had our best two free-throw shooters at the line only to have them miss. Every little play, every moment, had to go right for Kansas and wrong for us, and it did.

And then, after all that, it took a miracle, once-in-a-lifetime shot from Mario Chalmers to send the game into overtime.

We ended up losing 75–68, and all I remember about walking off the floor at the Alamodome was the numbness. We went from the pinnacle to "Oh, my gosh." And I'm telling you, it's a fast sensation. This thing was bam-bam-bam-bam—what in the world just happened?

As Kansas celebrated and their fans rejoiced, my team headed to the locker room, dejected and dismayed. We were as close as you could be—two minutes and twelve seconds from being national champs. Another few feet from being 40–0. That's the margin between glory and guilt. At the end of the day, we were chasing the stars and we bumped into the moon. We were that close.

As we all walked off that court—some of us with tears in our eyes, some with completely blank stares—I knew something that nobody else in our program knew: each and every one of us had just begun our own bounce back.

I also knew everyone was going to be looking to me for an answer—in the locker room, in the media room, and on the famed River Walk in San Antonio. They were going to turn to me and hope for an explanation or a justification. I never have a problem talking after a win or a loss, but this time was completely different from anything I'd ever experienced.

By the time I got into the locker room underneath the Alamodome's stands, I knew I had to provide leadership and guidance for everyone associated with our program. These were eighteen-, nineteen-, twenty-year-old kids, and you can be damn sure none of them had ever felt this horrible after a game in their lives. I had coaches, administrators, friends, and family who were all dealing with the devastation of the way we fell and the thump we made as we hit the ground.

I realized at that moment that I was not dealing with just my own shock and grief. I had to deal with everyone's—from players to fans to assistants. I was the leader for those thirty-eight record-setting wins, and I was the leader for the two losses as well. Did I want to run and hide? You bet. But I realized—and you need to realize—that you're not the only one feeling the pain and anguish. Everyone around you is hurting, and you better deal with them before you deal with yourself. That's what being a coach, an executive, a parent, a son, or a daughter is all about during trying times. If you show weakness over the setback you have encountered, everyone around you will sense that uncertainty and fear, and it will only make things worse.

I allowed myself about five minutes of introspection and regret in the coaches' locker room, and then I splashed some water on my face, adjusted my tie, and joined the players in their locker room.

There were tears, anger, and disbelief all around the room. The shock was setting in and so was the realization of what had happened. At that moment, I remember thinking that I wished I could have just done one thing to get them over the hump in the game, because I could see how they were suffering. I could feel it. We were all hurting—everyone associated with Tiger basketball. Shock causes pain, and that sting lingers.

If I had given in to that emotion, it would have started everybody's bounce back on the wrong foot. So I told my team exactly what I was feeling and let them know the hurt was normal.

"I don't want any of you to think you were the reason," I said to the young men in the locker room. "You did everything you were supposed to, and you put us in a position to win a national title. What happened out there is not on one person; it's on all of us, including me as the coach. At the end of the day with that kind of lead, it comes back to me.

"I am more proud of you guys than I've ever been," I said. "You gave me an unbelievable gift this whole season. We did things no other team has ever done in the history of college basketball. We were a dream team, and you cannot ever forget that. This was a dream season with a dream team. We energized and united our city.

"Does this hurt right now? Do you feel like crap?" I asked. "That's okay. That feeling will go away over time. Soon you're going to remember the twenty-six straight wins, the undefeated conference record, and the family we built throughout the year. Look around—you may never play with some of these guys again, but you will always have the experience and memories of what we accomplished over forty games."

The words were probably ringing hollow, but I knew they had to be said in order for everyone to be able to move on. I hugged all my guys and my incredible staff, and then I prepared to face the media.

> **PractiCal Point:** Remember, your trigger event will impact on others around you, so you need to be strong for them.

. . .

It's not likely that your bounce back will kick off with a press conference with a couple hundred anxious, on-deadline writers and TV and radio people begging for that one money quote they can use in their column, game story, or broadcast. For that, you should be thankful.

I couldn't avoid it though. The NCAA mandates coaches and selected players sit on the dais and answer media questions after a designated "cooling off" period. In a strange way, I knew that session would be an important step in our collective bounce back, as would the questions the rest of the team was answering in the locker room. It wasn't enough to be gracious in defeat; this kind of loss required me to be humble, forgiving, and empathetic.

"Hats off to Kansas. When you're up nine with 2:12 left, you're supposed to win the game, and that's my fault," I said in my opening statement. "I thought we were national champs, and that's the great thing about college basketball and sports. I'm really disappointed but so proud of my guys. You know, again, as a coach, when you're up five with whatever seconds left to go, you're supposed to win that game. So I take as much responsibility in this. I'm disappointed for my team. I wish there were a few more things we could have done there to make it easier for them at the end. But I'm proud of them. They did everything they were supposed to do really against the odds, and they did it, and they were there, and it slips. I mean, it's devastating to them."

I admit I was still kind of numb during that press conference. That happens. You're numb to it all in the minutes and hours after your "trigger event." I knew it was going to hit me like a ton of bricks the next day, realizing we'd had it in our grasp. I took a late walk with my staff on the River Walk after returning to the hotel and meeting with our fantastic fans and well-wishers.

I thought about what I had said to the media. With those words, I was doing a few things—first I was taking the burden off my team, which any good leader needs to do when the chips are down. It's not a time to point fingers or place blame. No one thing cost us the game; it was a perfect storm of everything going right for Kansas, and everything going wrong for us.

Another important element of those immediate minutes and hours after the loss was to make sure that I and everyone involved with the program gave due credit to Kansas. The Jayhawks, under Bill Self, proved what it means to play to the final buzzer and never give up hope. They had just mastered their own bounce back. There was no shame in losing to that team, which had several eventual NBA draft picks, and we had to make sure people understood what an accomplishment they had achieved. Our "failure" was their success.

Understand that people will begin assessing you for your next job, relationship, or business deal as soon as they see you are dealing with a pitfall. From the moment your trigger event happens, you need to put on a good face.

Admittedly, there's so much swirling when you are in the midst of a major life setback that you can't possibly react to everything in the appropriate way—unless you have been there before.

And I had.

CHAPTER 2

LEARNING FROM EXPERIENCE

YOUR FIRST BOUNCE BACK
IS THE HARDEST

B efore we can get too far into your bounce back, I think it's important for you to see some "game tape" of the two major public bounce backs that I have been through in the past decade. We've already touched on the Kansas game. Please realize these reviews are not done to get sympathy from you or to bore you with details of my life experiences. What I want you to understand is this: not only have I bounced back from major setbacks, I've had two very different kinds of bounce backs. My first, when I was fired by the NBA's New Jersey Nets, played out over several weeks and eventually months and years as I transitioned through all the bounce-back stages we will discuss over the course of this book.

For me, the circumstances of my firing by the Nets in March 1999 were much harder to deal with than my second trigger event (in the title game) because I had never had to bounce back from anything like that before. When the Nets fired me, I had just turned forty, and I was learning all about dealing with a sudden life change on the fly and under the eye of the vigilant New York sports media and a discerning fan base. Sure, I had close friends and mentors like Larry Brown helping me all along the way, but in those first hours, days, and weeks after the trigger event occurs, you feel like it's you against the world, and that can be an overwhelming sensation.

But with every bounce back you have, you grow and you begin to understand that you're far from alone in dealing with your setback. You also begin to understand that you are not going to have just one, two, or three bounce backs in your life. In fact, you're never going to be done transforming yourself, your career, and your relationships. It's worth keeping in mind that you learn the most about bouncing back when you are going through it.

I know the reason I was able to handle the 2008 Kansas loss so well was because I had been through the turmoil of the Ncts firing in 1999 when I got publicly humiliated and smashed and survived it. When dealing with the title game loss, I knew from the New Jersey experience that I would wake up the next day and that each day it would get a little better—even though it was going to take time. I had lived through one public humiliation and because of that, I knew I could handle the aftermath of the title game loss.

And you know what? I'll be even better prepared for the next time I get dealt a setback.

Every bounce back you have—or are affected by—in life, you have to learn from. You have to assess what has happened and use that assessment to better yourself.

Bounce backs are like individual games throughout the season. No two are exactly the same; some include sudden swings, while others follow a logical back-and-forth progression. In any given season, my teams will have blow-out wins where everything is clicking and nail-biter losses that could have gone either way. Sometimes the team improves over the course of one game, and sometimes it takes two or three contests to see the improvement.

Just as each game develops at its own pace, so, too, will your bounce back. After every game I sit down and assess my team through film study and discussion with my assistants. You, too, should assess your performance frequently throughout the bounce back process. You will be wise to lean on the Kitchen Cabinet you will compile in Practice Plan #1 at the end of this chapter. Most of all, you have to always be honest with yourself. It does no good to base your bounce back on beliefs and perceptions that led you here in the first place. I always ask my teams and my players to own their performances, and I'm going to expect you to do the same. For my teams, that means taking responsibility for everything—the good and the bad—on the court and in their lives.

You need to *own* your bounce back in much the same manner.

Are you with me? Good. Here's the game tape on the very beginning of my time with the Nets and the very end of my time in New Jersey; I'll show you the way I went over what happened and how I behaved so that you can see how it's done, and then it will be your turn.

• • •

In 1996, my eighth year at the University of Massachusetts in Amherst, we had an incredible journey that included wins in our first twenty-six straight games, a No. 1 ranking, and the school's first-ever appearance in the Final Four (which, as fate would have it, was played in the arena at the New Jersey Meadowlands complex). We lost in the national semifinals to Kentucky, but the accomplishments of that team will live forever in the annals of college basketball.

I was humbled that year to be named the national Naismith Men's College Coach of the Year. It was the culmination of a total rebuilding project that saw us go 193–71 (.731) in that span as we reached three

Sweet 16s, two Elite 8s and the Final Four. We went from one of the absolute worst programs in America (ranked 259th of 267 Division I schools in the 1980s) to one of the best.

Along the way, we captured the hearts and imaginations of an entire state, and we boosted the morale of a campus that had always been maligned as "ZooMass." I started there when I was twenty-nine and wet behind the ears. By the time I left, I had seen and done things I never imagined possible.

When that '96 season ended, the NBA's New Jersey Nets contacted me about becoming their next head coach. It was always in the back of my mind that someday I would love the opportunity to coach in the greatest league in the world, so the prospect certainly intrigued me. The Elite 8 campaign the year before gave me confidence I could accept the challenge if it were ever presented to me. When the Nets— and others—expressed interest, I had to listen.

What I heard blew me away. They were giving me the keys to the castle, and in addition to being the head coach, I would hold the titles of executive vice president and head of basketball operations. After some negotiating, we settled on a five-year deal worth $15 million. It was the kind of package that was unheard of at the time, and after thinking long and hard about it and talking it over with my wife, Ellen, and trusted friends, I accepted the position on June 5, 1996.

It was far from an easy decision. I was giving up a job at UMass I could have had the rest of my life to go to an organization considered a laughingstock among the professional leagues. The Nets were always mentioned in the same breath as the Los Angeles Clippers and Tampa Bay Buccaneers, and at that time that was some bad company to be lumped in with. The Nets were dysfunctional and ridiculed, and as far as NBA jobs went, it was probably one of the least attractive in the league.

The job scared away a lot of folks, but I saw it as a chance to do something similar to what we had done at UMass. I embraced the challenge of building a franchise into a playoff contender and invigorating the fan base. It would take a heck of a lot of work and some serious dedication by all involved, but I believed in my heart of hearts we could turn the Nets into a respected NBA franchise.

The first year wasn't easy; we went 26–56, but my second season with New Jersey we went 43–39 and made the playoffs as an eight seed. We were swept in three games by the Michael Jordan–led Chicago Bulls, but just making the playoffs in our second season in Jersey was a huge accomplishment. I'm not sure many people understood just how incredible it was. Put it this way: the Nets had finished under .500 in nine of the eleven seasons before I got there, and in five of those years the teams failed to win any more than twenty-six games. The franchise had not been out of the first round of the playoffs since 1984.

So, as you can imagine, I was feeling like we had things moving in the right direction. We were drawing well in terms of attendance, we had a new logo that fans embraced, and a new attitude that was palpable. A dedicated practice facility was being built, and free agents weren't as hesitant to consider the Nets as an option. It was about as much as anyone could have expected.

But labor unrest loomed, and in 1998 the NBA slogged its way through a messy lockout by its owners that prohibited the season from starting until February 1999. When it did commence, it was abbreviated from the usual eighty-two-game slate to a fifty-game schedule.

With that as the backdrop, we started off 2–10, and as is customary in professional sports, the whispers started circulating that my job was in danger.

I had a feeling that my firing was coming. We suffered through two losing streaks of six games, and by mid-March, I was already telling Ellen something was imminent. "Honey, I think we need to start preparing for what will be a very public and a very cruel process," I told her one winter night. "NBA people didn't like me when I came in because of the big contract I got, and they're going to delight in seeing me get dumped. We need to be ready."

In that regard, I was actually lucky. More often than not, you don't know you're about to have a trigger event that will turn your world upside down. But I knew my relationship with the new Nets' owners, president Michael Rowe, and general manager John Nash (whom I hired) had deteriorated; things were bad, and I had a feeling that we were past the point of being able to work things out. They were ready to make a change.

We'd started the season with high expectations and were coming off a playoff season. *Slam* magazine picked us to win the Eastern Conference for 1998–99, and other "experts" had high hopes for us as well. There was a bit of a buzz around us, and even that was significant because the franchise had always been a poor cousin to the big-city New York Knicks.

But the lockout had caused some extenuating circumstances, including an abbreviated training camp and a too-brief period of time to sign players and integrate them into our system. After a 1–1 start, Sammy Cassell, my starting point guard and one of the most fearless players I've ever coached, went down with an injury. Without a point guard in the NBA, you're spinning your wheels. We didn't have a capable backup, and Sammy's injury marked the beginning of the end for me.

I don't go over this to make excuses; those are facts of the situation. In your own bounce back, you have to be able to look at your situation objectively; even if it feels like it came out of the blue, evaluating it from a distance might show you there were warning signs you'll want to be able to look out for next time. As I said, the bottom line was we weren't winning, and as the losing continued, rumors intensified that I would be fired. In my case, I knew that it all comes down to wins and losses in the NBA. Even though we made the playoffs the year before (the first for the franchise in four seasons), we started off poorly, and I had a feeling that the writing was on the wall.

Things came to a head in mid-March of 1999. We were playing the Miami Heat, winners of fourteen of their last sixteen games under head coach Pat Riley. We had lost six straight by an average of eleven points. Before the noontime game with the Heat even started, one of the guys on the TV crew came over to me and said he was hearing I was getting "dinged" after the game.

Perfect, I thought. *The camera guy knows I'm getting fired before I do!*

We lost the game 102–76, and I never got up off the bench. We scored just fifteen points in the second quarter and sixteen in the fourth quarter. My center, Jayson Williams, who had averaged thirteen points a game the previous two seasons, scored two points and fouled out in twenty-seven minutes of play.

When the game ended, there was a knot of uncertainty in my stomach—a perfectly normal response to impending bad news. It wasn't a good feeling, but I knew I had to take my medicine.

As I walked into the tunnel and toward our locker room, my assistant, Johnny Davis, put his arm around me and said, "Fight for the job. You are the same coach who took us to the playoffs. Fight for the job!"

I didn't have a fight left in me, and I knew that the decision had been made. Two of the team's owners, Stan Gale and Finn Wentworth, brought me into the visiting coaches' locker room and explained their position. They wanted to go in a new direction, and they were going to hand the team over to another of my assistants, Don Casey. I told them I didn't agree with what they were doing and that I thought they were making a mistake. But they had already made their decision, and our talk was a mere formality.

I remember coming out of that meeting at the old Miami Arena, and there was barely a soul around except for the Nets' principal owner and managing partner at the time, Lewis Katz. He told me to follow him to a car they had waiting.

Now you've got to understand, I'm half in a daze as I'm following him through the empty arena. I hadn't ever been fired from anything. I mean, my old boss at Kansas, Larry Brown, used to fire me every other day when I was an assistant for him, but that's just Larry. I was in complete shock and quite honestly still trying to figure out what was going on.

My team was gone; they were already on their way to Toronto for a Tuesday game against the Raptors. As I walked across the playing floor as an ex–NBA coach, there were workers cleaning up, sweeping and stacking chairs. There was a guy on his knees, kneeling there in a pile of popcorn and spilled soda, and he was looking up at me, shaking his head and feeling bad for me.

That's about when it really hit me—the cleaning crew was taking pity on me!

I don't remember saying very much to Katz in the car to the airport or on the flight home to New Jersey. I was still trying to process it all. I was humiliated for sure, but even more so, I felt like I had been stripped of my identity. For most of my adult life, I had been known as "Coach Cal"; now all of a sudden, I was just Cal. Sometimes we don't realize how much our careers define our personalities, but when you experience a major setback, it becomes very clear. The official end of my Nets coaching career marked the beginning of my first bounce back, and to say I was a little confused in the aftermath would be an understatement. So many thoughts were swirling in my head: *Whom do I call? What will be the perception from outsiders? What are my options?* As we flew home to New Jersey, I thought about how the rabid New York media—always quick to pounce on a juicy firing—was probably relishing the chance to skewer me. There were plenty of writers and media people who wanted to see me get canned, so the owners weren't going to take too much guff for the move. The focus would be on me and my errors. People were just itching to see another college coach "fail" at the pro level, a mindset that still exists today and probably will until one of us breaks through and has significant success in the pros.

I also began to feel the anxiety that I now know can routinely accompany such traumatic changes. For me, the anxiety of not knowing what was next was probably the worst part of it. Then there was the anxiety of "Have the Nets damaged me so much from what they were saying during the run-up to the firing that I won't be able to get another job?" I didn't necessarily know if I would coach again. I really didn't.

But as the plane landed, I quickly tried to push those thoughts from my mind and think about what was really important. I said to myself, *If this is the worst thing that happens to me and my family, I'll be blessed.* I had a whole host of people just waiting to help me. I believed everything was going to be fine, and I knew the most important thing was to get my bounce back started off on the right foot. I wanted to be strong in the face of adversity and for my family. If I were a puddle, displaying fear or nervousness, it would be an awful message to send to those around me.

We all have the ability to stay positive, even when the chips are down. It comes from within, and I know it is within everyone. We just have to search for it and massage it out. I need you to now find that positivity within and bring it to the fore. Dig deep, and you will find it.

> **PractiCal Point:** Let the emotions run their course, and then focus on starting your bounce back with a positive attitude.

• • •

I got home to my house in Franklin Lakes, New Jersey, in the late hours of March 14. My children—Erin, Megan, and Bradley—were sleeping, but Ellen and I sat up and had a glass of wine while we talked over things.

I was still dealing with a lot of unfamiliar emotions that ranged from anger to fear to confusion. Throughout my career I had always made the "big" decisions; all of a sudden I was having a huge decision made for me. It was a completely new sensation for me, and I wasn't enjoying it at all.

The greatest thing Ellen did for me in those first few hours and days was to be frank with me. She didn't hide her feelings, and you would be well advised to make sure the closest people to you are doing the same.

Bluntly, Ellen told me she didn't think the NBA lifestyle was a good fit for young families like ours. "There's too many games [eighty-two] first of all," she told me. "In college you had thirty-five games, and we could all be there for most of them and be a part of the program. I miss that, John, and the kids do too."

I already knew this, but it was helpful to hear it again from Ellen. At UMass both Erin and Megan could come to most of our home games—many were on the weekend—and we lived very close to the Mullins Center in Amherst, where we played. It was easier for my family to be part of the "organization."

I missed a lot about the college lifestyle as well. Don't get me wrong; in business we all aspire to work with the best, and that's what the NBA represents for me. I don't regret for one second the decision to leave UMass and go to the Nets; I learned and grew and matured throughout my time there, and I can safely say I wouldn't be the coach I am today without that experience. But I didn't feel that way overnight.

Ellen reemphasized she wasn't keen on having me pursue another NBA job. "The NBA is too unpredictable," she told me. "It's like you're in the military, moving from base to base!"

Her point was well taken, and I was pretty sure I wasn't going to get another shot at a head job in the NBA anytime soon. Ex–college coaches usually don't get second chances in the pros—especially not right away. Tim Floyd (Iowa State) got two head jobs, first with the Chicago Bulls and then with the New Orleans Hornets, and wound up back in college at USC. Lon Kruger (Illinois) went to the Atlanta Hawks for three years and then wound up at UNLV. None of them lasted a full four years, and none has been back to the NBA since.

Soon after Ellen and I had that talk, I had some time alone to think over things, and I came to a very important realization. It's one that you need to recognize early and keep fresh in your mind during your bounce back:

Nothing was going to happen overnight. Bouncing back from

this will be a gradual process. **Championship organizations aren't built in a day or even a week. Your bounce back isn't going to happen at the snap of a finger.**

Whatever setback you are going through—job loss, relationship strife, health issues—know that it will take a length of time to play out. Divorces unfold over weeks and months. A professional career is built over decades, not days. Health issues evolve over time. Virtually every life experience is a compilation of many events over a series of weeks, months, and years. There are no magic wands to solve serious issues, and you have to accept that early, or you are just fooling yourself.

People will deal with their situation as best they can. Let me tell you this: during those first few days after the Nets firing, I was in my own world at times. There was no specific mood to it, but I had ups and downs and in-betweens. There were times I'd be back in my home office, and I would make lists about things I had done right and things I had done wrong. I would make lists of people I knew I could call. I think I started making lists about my lists! But those jottings helped, and I'd encourage you to get your thoughts in writing at the first available moment.

Here is where we need to reemphasize a very important point about these early days and weeks of your bounce back. This isn't meant to scare you; it's meant to let you know the phases you're going through are perfectly normal.

Realize you are in the beginning stages in this journey, and there are several shifts and swings you will experience. Experts tell us there will be—among other things—periods of:

Isolation—You may want to "go into hiding." You won't and don't see anyone. You remove yourself from technology and go "underground." It's a natural reaction to seek solitude when things go astray. The danger is when that isolation becomes permanent or delays your forward progress. I'm not telling you to always need to be surrounded by people, but I am telling you the only thing being alone is going to do in the long run is make you more miserable.

I only allowed myself a couple of days of isolation after the Nets firing, and really, I didn't have much more than a few hours of alone time after the Kansas loss. If you are able to keep yourself busy—and your mind occupied—early on, the isolation stage will not be damaging to you. The importance of human contact is huge. It's not a bad idea to seek friends outside your immediate circle who may not know what the circumstances of your trigger event are. That way you won't be forced into talking about it nonstop.

Regret/Bargaining—Maybe you will think there are certain things you could have done to save yourself. Or perhaps you rue certain decisions you made for you or your business. Those are perfectly normal thoughts to encounter. When I was let go by the Nets, I started thinking of things I could have done differently—my sideline demeanor could have been better; I could have tried to gain more allies in the new front office. I mighta, coulda, shoulda . . .

The bargaining can manifest itself in different ways, and all it does is get you deeper in the quicksand of despair. You may bargain with yourself that if you can be strong enough to get through this rough patch, you will do things differently next time. A husband gets caught cheating on his wife, his wife wants a divorce, and the husband immediately starts negotiating. *"I'll never do it again, honey. It was a one-time thing. I'll buy you a new car and we can move on."*

Or *"Sorry, boss; I'll be more careful on my expenses. I'll work overtime. I'll travel more."* We've all heard it before.

Please, stop it. What's done is done, and you need to accept the consequences of what has happened.

I fought the regret after both the Nets and, maybe more so, the Kansas game, because there was a definite if/then order to the way things played out on the court. But in both cases I realized it did no good for me to constantly try to relive the past. It was over. The die had been cast. The best thing I could do with those regrets was learn from them and do my best to make sure they didn't happen in my next job.

Anger—This might accompany your regrets, or it may show itself in different ways. One of the best ways I know to get the anger out is to do some form of physical activity. When I was younger—and had my original hip!—I would jog every day. Now I speed walk a couple of miles each day. For you, it might be going to the gym, riding your bike, or even doing yoga.

Whatever it is, funnel that anger into the activity, and let it escape from your body and your mind.

Frustration—There's a tendency to want everything to be "fixed" in days. But the reality is, it's going to take weeks, months, and maybe even years to really get over the pain you are feeling. Don't let the frustration overcome you, and don't let it get in the way of your goals.

My biggest frustration after the New Jersey experience was the feeling that my future job prospects would be hindered by the way the dismissal went down. After the Kansas game, my frustration stemmed from not having been able to do more from the sideline and from seeing such a wonderful season end in such a crushing manner.

Depression—The National Institute of Mental Health estimates that "26.2 percent of Americans ages 18 and older suffer from a diagnosable mental disorder in a given year. When applied to the 2004 U.S. Census . . . this figure translates to 57.7 million people."

I don't claim to know much about depression, but I've read and heard enough to know how debilitating and crippling it can be. In a 2004 *USA Today* Health article, Terry Bradshaw spoke of his own clinical depression: "I could not bounce back from my divorce—emotionally—I just could not bounce back," Bradshaw said. "With any bad situations I'd experienced before—a bad game or my two previous divorces—I got over them. This time I just could not get out of the hole. The anxiety attacks were frequent and extensive. I had weight loss, which I'd never had before. I couldn't stop crying. And if I wasn't crying, I was angry, bitter, hateful and mean-spirited. I couldn't sleep—couldn't concentrate. It just got crazy."

After being diagnosed in the 1990s, Bradshaw attacked his problem the way he used to attack defenses with his arm—head on. "Depression is a physical illness," he said. "The beauty of it is that there are medications that work. Look at me. I'm always happy-go-lucky, and people look at me and find it shocking that I could be depressed."

But he was, he recognized it, and he dealt with the disease.

If you think you're displaying signs of depression—and they can manifest in many ways—you need to seek professional help sooner rather than later. Depression can be treated the same way other diseases are, but not until you recognize it and begin to address the problems with treatment. A valuable place to start is at the National Institute of Mental Health's website (see: Cal's Bounce-Back Resources, Appendix B).

All of these stages are perfectly normal during the course of your bounce back. It's how you deal with each step along the way that will determine the success of your bounce back. It took a certain length of time to get you into this position, and it can't be undone or solved in minutes or days or weeks. *Be patient.*

> **PractiCal Point:** Speak honestly and openly about what you're going through, and accept the fact that your bounce back is in an embryonic stage.

• • •

That first day after the firing was a tough one. I'd be lying to you if I said I was out of bed the next morning all bright-eyed and bushy-tailed. I wanted to stay under the covers, believe me. But what kind of example would that have been to my kids? What would Ellen have thought? It would have been a huge mistake to start my bounce back from a prone position under the blankets.

I knew that my kids and Ellen were looking to me to provide guidance during this time period. If they saw me get down and discouraged, then they would get down and discouraged. So I never allowed the anxiety I was feeling to creep into my home life.

The girls were young, but they knew what was going on. We recently found this letter that Megan had to write to the teachers she was going to have the next year in fourth grade. (Trust me, her spelling has gotten a *lot* better since then—she'll be a sophomore at Kentucky in 2009.)

240 Hidden Pond Path
Frankline Lakes NJ 07417
May 26, 1999

Dear Fourth Grade teachers,
I'm looking forward to going into forth grade. My dad just got fired from coching the Nets. We are now cheering for the Knicks. I like teasts a lot. I have brown hair and brown eyes.
From Megan Calipari

That was how Megan handled it. "We are now cheering for the Knicks." Isn't that great? She knew something had happened, but she wasn't going to dwell on it. She had already moved on. We'd all be well served by having a little bit of "kid" in us during our bounce backs.

Beyond that childlike attitude, you also need to acknowledge the bounce back process is going to most likely have a rocky beginning. Because of that, it is so very important that you don't allow early emotional setbacks to derail the tracks you are about to lay.

This point was reemphasized to me by Roberta "Bobbie" LaPorte, a UMass graduate with an MBA from Harvard who now lives in San Francisco. I became aware of Bobbie when a friend forwarded me an email of an online program she was offering UMass alumni to help them through career change.

Bobbie's got a great story. She had worked in high-level positions at IBM, General Electric, and UnitedHealthcare Group before starting a consulting firm, RAL & Associates (www.bobbielaporte .com), which provides leadership- and career-development services. As Bobbie explained it, she has "worked with hundreds of individuals to find the 'best next step' in their professional lives and take charge of their careers."

Bobbie is now a financial advisor with Morgan Stanley in San Francisco. I leaned on her for help with various parts of this book, and you will hear from her throughout.

Bobbie's advice on career comebacks serves as a universal truth for almost any type of bounce back.

In addition to career coaching, Bobbie is an accomplished triathlete, and she puts a lot of stock in combining a healthy mind with a healthy body, especially during times of bounce back. But first, she told me, you need to get through the "grieving."

"When a demotion or termination or some type of career shakeup happens, I usually suggest to people they let it happen for some period of time anyway," she said. "Because they really need to let the emotional part of that [play out]. There's also the disappointment and sense of failure—whether it was their fault or not—that sometimes comes with a setback. There are all kinds of ranges of emotions people go through. It can be beneficial to talk to somebody, maybe a psychologist even, and work through it all. These are powerful emotions being experienced."

This will sound strange, but sometimes it's easier to handle this grieving when dealing with a death—the person is gone, you reconcile your thoughts, and there is some closure. In other types of bounce backs such as breakups or job loss, the person(s) or company remains as a constant reminder, making it tougher to reach that point of closure.

Still, that closure must come, and even if it comes in slow, gradual steps, you need to allow it to wash over you. Let go of past events, know they cannot be changed, and above all else, start your bounce back with an attitude that doesn't just say, "I think I can," but instead screams, "I know I will."

> **PractiCal Point:** Take stock of what has happened, and be prepared to attack your bounce back with passion and a positive attitude—no matter what.

· · ·

Throughout this "playbook" for your bounce back, I will include "practice plans" I'd like you to complete as we go along. Even if you think the drill is not something you will benefit from, I ask you to still do it. Everything I do in my practices is for a specific reason, and every drill I ask you to partake in is also for a specific reason—even if that reason isn't apparent to you now.

There are no time limits or expectations for when you will move from one step to another. My practice plans never include time limits for each part of the practice. If we're all understanding the concept and performing it to my satisfaction, we move on to the next drill. If the team looks confused or isn't executing properly, we work on it until it is no longer an issue. Sometimes we will come back to certain aspects the next day or a week later to ensure the skills have been retained and processed in the minds of the players. The only expectation is that you will give your best effort every day and maintain a positive outlook:

These Practice Plans are available for downloading at www.coachcalbounceback.com.

PRACTICE PLAN #1

IDENTIFY YOUR KITCHEN CABINET

EMPHASIS OF THE DAY: Identifying your Kitchen Cabinet

During my trip to China with a team of Conference USA all-stars (made up mostly of my Memphis team) in the summer of 2008, I took with me the book *The Success Principles* from best-selling author Jack Canfield. (Jack , as you probably know, was the cocreator of the popular *Chicken Soup for the Soul*.) In the book, Jack calls his close, personal advisors "staff members," but the concept is exactly the same as my Kitchen Cabinet. (The term was first used widely in reference to President Andrew Jackson's trusted pack of advisors, most of whom were outside his group of "official" advisors.) I really loved what Jack wrote about the need for these types of advisors, and I'm going to share it with you here:

Every high achiever has a powerful team of personal advisors to turn to for assistance, advice, and support. In fact, this team is so critical, it pays to begin assembling them early on in your success journey.

Regardless of whether you own a business, work for someone else, or stay home and raise your children, you need personal advisors to answer questions, help you plan, ensure that you make the most of life's efforts, and more.

At this early stage of your bounce back, you need to take some time and determine who it is you are going to lean on most heavily in the coming weeks and months. Your family is obviously part of that group, and close friends as well. But what I really want you to do now is look beyond those people and honestly contemplate and identify the people who will make up your Kitchen Cabinet (or KC for short).

These are the confidants and supporters in your life who have always been there for you, through thick and thin. They've shared in your triumphs and felt the pain of your losses. It's a select group that each of us already has but which many of us never take the time to identify.

You want to make sure to include a cross-section of friends and associates who are not afraid to tell you things you may not want to hear. When I was weighing the choice between staying in Memphis or going to Kentucky in late March 2009, my KC was so incredibly important, I can't even tell you.

I can tell you that my KC is constantly evolving. I don't necessarily eliminate any members, but I have found there have been people who have become valued confidants, whom I find myself leaning on more than some of my prior KC members. It's fine to have a shifting Kitchen Cabinet list, and it makes perfect sense—as you move to different locations, take on new projects, or discover new interests, you are going to need a different compilation of folks whom you can turn to.

PURPOSE

This is going to do a few things for you. First, it will give you a starting point of whom you can call in these early days of your bounce back. Second, the list is going to be a constant reference point for you at different stages of your bounce back. It will remind you, even in your lowest moments, that there are members of your support system who will be there for you at any time of day whatever the size of the problem you encounter in your bounce back. The KC will be a group you can lean on at various times throughout your bounce back, and, when used properly, they will begin to embrace your bounce back as their own and revel in the success you will ultimately have.

You are not alone, and there are people who are yearning to help you. Some people need you to ask for the help first, and others will soon be offering it. It's your job to accept the help and make them all part of your bounce-back team.

Knowing that, once you settle on your KC, you can begin to reach out to this core group and let them know what you will need out of them. You will ask them to be as tough on you as I am with my teams—all the while understanding that "tough love" is exactly what you need to move from this low point to the summit you will soon be looking down from.

DRILL

Make a list of people you feel would qualify for your Kitchen Cabinet. The list can be of any length, but the shorter the better; eventually you will narrow the list to between three and six people. These are most likely going to be the closest of your allies, and it probably won't include a close relative (although it can). **Do not** include the coddlers in your life. God bless them, but the people who are going to be of most help to you are the ones who have an objective take on your situation and have no fear of telling you *exactly* what is on their minds.

Think of the people who have always given you guidance and support throughout your life. It can be a childhood friend, a former boss, a mentor, an ex-coworker, a business associate, almost anyone who has made a positive impact on you during your life—but again, there cannot be a bunch of yes-men on your list. Be honest with yourself; more likely than not, the confidants you are reluctant to include are the very ones who need to be on the list. If there's the slightest possibility of tea and sympathy from a potential cabinet member, cross that one off immediately.

You need to include people who will challenge you and not be afraid to tell you things you don't want to hear. If you want otherwise, you can go to your mother, father, spouse, sister, brother, dog, or cat. These people on your KC are *not* going to rub your back and bake you cookies.

Make sure the list includes people of high character with good morals; be sure you have a diversity of backgrounds and specialties within your KC—a rock band doesn't need two drummers, and you don't need two people who bring exactly the same thing to the table. Just as my Kentucky team needs depth and breadth of players—guards, forwards, bangers, finesse players, contributors—your KC needs players ready to serve different roles.

I'd strongly suggest including at least one person who has an intimate knowledge of your specific industry or dilemma (a veteran of the wars, so to speak); another who has been through something similar to your situation (someone who has lived through what you're about to experience); a person who is extremely grounded and realistic (you don't need dreamers and schemers clouding your judgment); the biggest "tough love" associate you have (a no-BS person who won't be afraid to tick you off if you're being stubborn or close-minded); and it's also advisable, when possible, to have at least one member of the opposite gender (often, perspective from the opposite sex can be quite enlightening).

Also, be sure that your KC members are at least familiar with one another and will be able to work in conjunction with one another on your behalf. You want your cabinet to act as a team, so if there winds up being members who don't know one another, it will be your responsibility to introduce them.

After you get your initial list of names written down, trim off at least two people you determine to be just a bit *too* nice— the ones who might have even the slightest tendency to give you the "Aw, Johnny, I know how you feel." It's not to say those people can't be part of your bounce back, but it is to say that you recognize you will need people giving you more vinegar than sugar.

WATCH ME FIRST

On the next page, you will find the Kitchen Cabinet list I made shortly after I was fired by the Nets, and a brief description of why I chose each person. You, too, should—as I have done— make some notes on why you chose each person, to confirm you have a good cross-section of critical thinkers, business minds, and spiritual figures. (I realize I have some fairly high-profile people on my list, but stature or wealth has no effect on your Kitchen Cabinet. I have been lucky enough to meet and befriend some amazingly wise people through my career. If you're having trouble filling your list, there are always books—like this one!—that can fill the void. Harvey Mackay, Ken Blanchard, and Bob Rotella are all bestselling authors whose writings I have turned to at numerous times in my life.)

If you discover two members are too similar in personality and approach, you may want to consider one of your "cuts" or think of someone new entirely to replace one of them. This has to be a list you are comfortable with and one that includes the allies you know will be the most constructively critical at all times. You have to be comfortable that you can call any of them at any time and know each will be willing and able to help you with anything.

CAL'S KITCHEN CABINET (ALPHABETICAL):

Ken Blanchard—*A great business mind and the author of* The One Minute Manager. *I met Ken during the early 1990s at UMass. I've always admired his bright outlook and his spirituality. His approach to problem solving and his rational thinking are elements everyone needs from at least one of their KC members.*

Larry Brown—*A mentor, a friend, a basketball expert, and a confidant. Coach Brown knew better than almost anyone in the business what was in store for me during my revitalization. He's been through changes in his career and with each* new opportunity he's been able to add to his Hall of Fame legacy. I knew he'd be able to guide me through the land mines, and I knew he would also be someone who would make calls of recommendation and support on my behalf. He is probably the Kitchen Cabinet member who will give me the most "tough love."

James "Bruiser" Flint—*"Bru" is like a brother to me. He was with me at UMass and eventually took over that program when I left for the Nets job. For a long time at UMass, others would call him my driver because he would always join me for long road trips to visit recruits or tour the state to promote our university. Those car rides brought us together in ways I can't even explain. We would talk about basketball, sure. But mostly we talked about life and the morals and values we wanted to always display and instill within our families and with our players. I have always trusted Bru's gut instincts and his honesty like almost no one else's.*

Joe Malone—*The former state treasurer of Massachusetts, Joe has been through the wars of the Commonwealth's cutthroat political system. We met while I was at UMass, and he has been especially great at guiding me through my dealings with the media. Joe also has the ability to always keep me positive and upbeat. He's seen everything and is levelheaded no matter what is going on. You always want a couple of those people on your KC—ones who aren't shocked easily and who won't panic even when you might.*

Bob Marcum—*My former athletic director at UMass, Bob has had a remarkable career as an athletic administrator. He* *did a highly educational stint as athletic director at the University of South Carolina and had a successful career in the highest levels of college athletics as well as two stints as a NASCAR motor speedway executive. There's not much Bob hasn't seen, and he's been through bounce backs of his own, always coming out vindicated and stronger. He's a straight shooter and has the unique ability to assess situations quickly and offer solutions with conviction and prescience.*

Bob Rotella—*A highly respected motivational author and speaker who has worked with some of the PGA golf tour's—and major sports'—most recognizable figures. His psychological-based assessments and instructions are invaluable, and I make it a point every year to have Bob come and speak with my team about the power of positivity and a proper mind-set. He has always been able to bring me down to earth even in the toughest of times, and he constantly emphasizes the need for me to "stay in love with myself."*

CHAPTER 3

GET OUT FROM UNDER THE COVERS

YOU ARE NOT ALONE

I'm not going to lie to you; these first few days and weeks of your bounce back will not be easy. Because of the constant learning and experimenting you are going through at this early point in your bounce back, I compare these next few chapters of the book to the nonconference schedule my team plays in the first couple of months every season. It's during this portion of our schedule when I am able to evaluate and learn about my team's strengths and weaknesses.

For you, this "nonconference slate" will be the time when you evaluate your own situation, discover your inner strength, and establish the foundation that your bounce back will be built upon. As with my team, you will be facing "opponents" you don't often see, and many of the experiences will be a bit foreign to you. That's okay and normal—by getting through these challenges, you will be at your very best for the start of conference play and eventually for the postseason.

Some of those oddities you face may be the mornings when you wake up and all you want to do is stay under the covers and hide from the world, for a very long time.

I distinctly remember a few mornings like that. I would stare up at the ceiling and ruminate over every little thing. I was worrying about what was being written about me in the newspapers and what was being said about me on talk radio or TV. Even if your situation isn't as public as mine was, you're probably wondering what others are thinking or saying about you. But it's not healthy to dwell on those things.

I worked hard not to let those thoughts dominate my mind. I won't lie; the experience hurt, and I had some anger to deal with. But none of the events, words, or gestures that led to your situation can be changed. The rumors and whispers about your breakup or your fall from grace are going to be out there because people love to gossip. The worst thing you can do is try and fight those disparaging comments you think may be circulating.

It seems like this kind of nastiness happens more when relationships fail, such as with divorce or separation, and, believe me, I've known people who have been put through the wringer with ugly divorces. There's a coach at a school in Tennessee who split from his wife only to have her open a hair-and-nail salon near his campus called Alimony's a year after their divorce. The ex-wife justified the name and the business by telling the *Knoxville News Sentinel,* "I want [clients] to have had a nice experience and see that you can go through some horrible stuff and come out on top. [Divorce] isn't the end of the world. It feels like it at first, but it's not." She even put a red heart to dot the *i* in *Alimony's* to "be that extra pain in the ass," she told the paper.

You just have to rise above them and not let them drag down your bounce back. That nastiness and pettiness are out of your control completely, and there's no sense in dwelling on them. Don't bring yourself down to that level.

You will be much better off using your time constructively and productively. That is why, during these early days of your bounce back, it is vital to maintain the right frame of mind and be sure you are not allowing the "what ifs" to creep in. You may have regrets and unanswered questions, but now is not the time to focus on those issues. I'm not telling you to ignore what has brought you to this place in your career or your life; I am telling you not to get bogged down in the small stuff.

I constantly emphasize to my teams that they need to "major in the major." There are things that are important—that we have some say in—and all the other stuff is minor. What happens after you have moved on from the bad situation you were in is inconsequential to you now. We can't control people's opinions of us; the only thing we can do is behave in ways that are above reproach.

> **PractiCal Point:** You have to move forward
> and not look backward.

. . .

There is an acceptable time for grieving over your loss or major change, but you will be at a disadvantage if you let that period linger too long.

"I think two or three weeks for most people is enough time for them to process what was happened," career coach Bobbie LaPorte told me. "That's about enough time for a person to feel bad and get sympathy from their family and supporters.

"However, for other people it could be a couple of months before they can come to terms with what they are going through," she said. "It might take them weeks before they can 'get out from under the covers,' or make phone calls, and I'd say that's not healthy. A lot of it depends on the individual, his or her personality and view of life. People who are generally negative and say, 'I'm the victim,' or, 'Woe is me,' are going to be very hard-pressed to take an active role in creating the next opportunity for themselves."

In fact, Bobbie said in her consulting business she wouldn't even work with those kinds of people. "I know it's going to be a losing battle," she said.

I knew I didn't want to be one of those Negative Nellies, and for me, one of the most helpful realizations in those early days after the Nets firing was that I needed to create normalcy in my life. All of this will sound clichéd, but it really is the truth. You need a routine.

Get up every day, and when your feet hit the floor, say "Thank you." Look at each day as a new opportunity and each new opportunity as a new day in your bounce back. Shower, get dressed, have breakfast, and attack your bounce back as if it were your full-time job—because it is. As hard as you worked in your last job or as much devotion as you put into your failed relationship, that's the amount of effort that needs to be put into your resurgence.

After the Nets firing, I began to develop a regular, daily routine. My son, Bradley, was at a great age (two years old) at the time, and I was able to really enjoy him and the girls, who were eleven (Erin) and nine (Megan). Family is a great thing to immerse yourself in, but it's not the only thing. You also need activities and projects to occupy your time. I started working out regularly and was able to play more golf than I ever had in my life. Running was always something I had used for both my physical and emotional well-being, and I committed myself to daily runs. I started lifting weights, and in a short time I was looking better physically, and that began to help my emotional state. The weights toned my body, and the runs cleared my mind.

One guy I know who was going through a breakup started doing Bikram Yoga, which is a set of twenty-six yoga poses performed over ninety minutes in a studio heated to 110 degrees. He said it was the best workout of his life; he not only shed some extra weight, but he found some inner peace through the yoga. He started doing it three times a week and did it throughout his bounce back. It became an integral part of his resurgence, in fact.

Hey, whatever works, right?

Developing regular routines and healthy habits are vital during this time period because it gives structure to your life. Whether you'd been coaching or running a sales staff or doing manual labor, you were always running around from this practice to that game or from this event to that meeting.

All of a sudden, I remember realizing I didn't have anywhere to be. When you're immersed in your job, your family, your relationship, or whatever has been thrown into turmoil, you are constantly kept moving by those activities or people. It leaves little time to dwell on things that therefore aren't allowed to get magnified.

When you are going through a bounce back, there is likely to be a lot of downtime and moments for reflection. True, some of those looks back may be needed and may even be healthy in small doses. However, those moments can also lead to negativity seeping into your head, and you don't want that. Wishing bad luck on the Nets wasn't necessary for me—Ellen was doing enough of that for both of us. She would cheer when they lost and check out chat rooms to see how angry the Nets fans were getting. Ellen's attitude made me smile because I knew that was her way of coping and supporting me. That's okay too. Spouses often become more bitter in vexing situations—it's a way for them to cope, and as long as it doesn't get nasty or persist, it's okay.

I'm telling you that by developing a regular pattern of activity for myself, I was able to reestablish some routines in my life that served as a solid base for my ultimate bounce back. Even on the bad days, I was getting up out of bed, saying, "Thank you." I told myself that I was grateful for whatever happened and that, good or bad, the process was allowing me an opportunity to learn and grow.

That's exactly what you need to be thinking at this stage of your bounce back.

> **PractiCal Point:** Develop a regular routine to keep you grounded and looking forward.

. . .

Now is a good time to talk about perspective and the role it will play in your bounce back. Once you are able to step back and look objectively at your situation, you are going to be in a much better position to begin your resurgence.

When I was fired from the Nets, I felt that my firing was the worst and most public and most humiliating that anyone had ever experienced. You may be feeling similar emotions regarding your circumstances.

Nothing could be further from the truth, however. You are not alone.

The average American will go through *at least* two job changes in his or her life. More than half of all marriages end in divorce, and that number goes up if it's a second marriage. House foreclosures, credit-card debt, and insolvency have risen to astonishing levels in the past two years. In fact, as we began the calendar year 2009, the unemployment rate was at a sixteen-year high of 7.2 percent according to the Bureau of Labor Statistics. That meant 11.1 million Americans were unemployed, almost 50 percent more than in 2007. The recession that began in '07 shows few signs of abating, and the nation has been braced for a long crawl back to prosperity.

At the time the BLS report was released, then-president-elect Barack Obama said the statistics were "real lives, real suffering, real fears."

Those realities underscore my premise that no one goes through life unscathed—no matter how rich, how smart, how talented, or how fortunate one may be. White collar, blue collar, or no collar, there is an undeniable commonality to the raw emotion that strikes people when they are knocked on their rear ends in a jarring and stunning way. Did I have financial security when the Nets let me go? Yes. But that didn't mean I wasn't shaken and uncertain of my future, much the way you may be right now. For the first time in my adult life, I wasn't "Coach" anymore, and it shook me to my core.

It's irrelevant whether you're a laborer making minimum wage or a corporate executive with a corner office. When the sudden realization of job loss hits you—or any life-altering event unfurls—you are crippled and sent to your knees. You feel like a failure, and you lose your identity.

You are not a failure, and your identity will be what you make it. Divorce, foreclosure, illness—anything that you are being affected by—has happened to someone, somewhere, and you have to understand that all those people got through the adversity. You need to have the proper perspective. This is no time to let emotion cloud your judgment.

How about this one? Henry Ford—the inventor of the assembly line and one of America's most successful and respected businessmen ever—endured a complete failure that hardly ever gets mentioned when speaking of Ford's career.

In a nutshell, during the late 1920s, Ford decided he would try and break the rubber manufacturing monopoly of Great Britain and its Indochina rubber plantations. In his early sixties, Ford concocted a plan to grow rubber trees in the Amazon where most of the world's rubber had originally come from. Ford had a lot to gain by controlling rubber growing and manufacturing as it was mainly his automobiles that were demanding the rubber for tires.

Ford's vision was gargantuan as he dreamed of building an American utopia in the middle of the Amazon rain forest. He didn't just want to create the largest rubber plantation in the world; he wanted to build a fully functioning industrial city.

Ford workers from the States were relocated, as a power plant, a modern hospital, a church, homes, a hotel, a library, a golf course, and other American amenities sprouted up in the middle of the Amazon. Ford's Model Ts populated the streets, and rubber plants filled the plantations.

However, instead of relying on botanists to make sure the seedlings would grow and produce tons of rubber, Ford relied on his own engineers. The trees were planted too close together, the restrictions placed on workers resulted in unrest among the workforce, and Fordlandia never got on track the way Ford had hoped.

Suffice to say, it was an epic failure, and some estimates put the cost of the experiment in today's dollars at $200 million or more.

Think about that—Henry Ford, the father of the automobile industry and one of the most important figures in U.S. history, suffered an incredibly embarrassing public failure late in his life. Still, Ford was resilient enough to bounce back and find further success with his Ford Motor Company, including the company's introduction of the V-8 and the patenting of plastic-body autos. Ford was a risk taker and was strong enough to endure any kind of setback—it's probably why most of us have never heard of Fordlandia.

The business world, of course, has no shortage of CEOs and leaders who were kicked to the curb, only to come back and find prosperity in another role, with another company. In Harvey Mackay's bestselling book *We Got Fired,* he tells the stories of people like Donald Trump, who has been pronounced "done" more times than he's uttered the words *You're fired* on his TV show.

There's Lee Iacocca, who was fired by Ford before turning competitor Chrysler around in the 1980s. Or how about Bernie Marcus, who was fired as CEO of a home-improvement chain before starting The Home Depot? Larry King, the undisputed king of talk shows, was fired from a radio, TV, and writing job in the early 1970s. Apple cofounder Steve Jobs was ousted from the company in 1985—by the very man he had hired to run the company! McDonald's founder Ray Kroc was $100,000 in debt and selling blenders in his late thirties before becoming a millionaire in his fifties. The list goes on and on and is ever increasing.

My dad, Vince, has always told me, "Johnny, it's not quite as bad as it seems, and it's not quite as good as it seems. Somewhere in the middle falls reality, so keep things in perspective!" I'm often reminded of that when I think of this story regarding my older sister, Terri, who went away to school at Penn State. We hadn't heard from her in about a month, and one night, we sat down to dinner, and my mom said, "There's a letter from Terri." She opened it and began to read it:

"Dear Mom, Dad, Lea, and John,

All here in Happy Valley is fine. I love the school, my classes, and my new friends. My dorm did burn to the ground, and I lost all my clothes, books, and belongings. All is okay, as I went to Goodwill, borrowed books, and moved into an off-campus apartment.

My new roommate, Jim, is quite a fellow. He has been out of rehab for six months and has been doing fine. I do want to apologize to all of you for not inviting you to the wedding, but it happened rather quickly. I also want to congratulate you, Mom and Dad, on becoming grandparents, and I know you will be the best ever! Lea and John, you guys will be great as aunt and uncle, I just know it.

Your Loving daughter,

Terri

P.S. Dad, all of the above is a lie. I failed chemistry, and I wanted you to keep things in perspective."

We all got a kick out of the letter at dinner that night, but the lesson from Terri's letter still resonates today.

It also brings me to another simple but effective strategy for dealing with your situation: laughter.

There have actually been studies done on the benefit of laughter for those going through tough times, and it is consistently proven that laughter is good for healing. At its simplest form, laughter puts a smile on your face, and that alone can put you on the road back.

I read about a well-respected editor and writer, Norman Cousins, who spent thirty years as editor of the *Saturday Review*. Cousins suffered from a condition that deteriorated his spine, leaving his chance of survival grim according to doctors in 1964. But Norman read up on his disease and became an active participant in his own bounce back. In his book *Anatomy of an Illness,* Norman details how he went from a hospital room to a hotel room and altered his prescription-medication regimen based on his research. Maybe more important, Norman got himself a reel-to-reel projector and a tape player and immersed himself in both the TV show *Candid Camera* and a host of old Marx Brothers movies. (I've had cancer-patient friends tell me that the Three Stooges work wonders for their states of mind!)

Cousins claimed he was overtaken by a state of euphoria, and in less than a month he was back at work and recovering. He lived another quarter of a century and became a huge proponent of the benefits of laughter in offsetting pain.

I remember after the Nets situation when I would watch *Saturday Night Live* or *Seinfeld* and would feel like I was being given a break from thinking about everything that was swirling in my world. It was an escape that afforded me the chance to focus on nothing but silly humor.

There will also be a point in your bounce back—maybe not right now—when it will also be constructive for you to display some self-deprecating humor about your circumstance. I've always been able to poke fun at myself, but I really employed the technique more after the Kansas loss than with the Nets deal.

This is a true story, and my son, Bradley, who was twelve at the time it happened, can attest to it. Bradley and I had gone to New York City for the July 2008 Major League Baseball All-Star Game at Yankee Stadium. As you may know, New York sports fans aren't exactly bashful about voicing their opinions. I love going on WFAN, the sports radio station in New York, because all the callers and even the hosts are so passionate about their teams and sports in general.

Anyway, we were walking around the All-Star fest that accompanies all the big sporting events now, and every few minutes there would be some wise guy walking by us who would give me the time-out signal, or another guy would be slapping his wrist to indicate "you should have fouled." Some wise guys yelled out, "Get a T.O., Coach Cal," in their best Dick Vitale voices. But they were all good-natured about it, and I took it as it was intended—a subtle jab from passionate sports fans. It was actually good for Bradley to see me laughing about it, I think. He had taken the Kansas loss hard—as had the girls and Ellen; we were three months away from it now, and it was healthy to realize that game wasn't the end of the world. No game is, and no personal loss, regardless of the pain, is going to stop the sun from rising again.

I now tell that story of my visit to Manhattan all the time, because it really does a great job of illustrating how important it is to laugh—both at others and at yourself—during this valley in your life.

> **PractiCal Point:** Maintain perspective, and a good sense of humor won't be far behind.

• • •

As much as I am going to coach you on using those around you to help you through your bounce back, it's at this time when we should probably focus on you and you alone. Yes, you need to put on a brave face for everyone around you, and, yes, you need to be soliciting advice from your trusted friends and associates. But first and foremost, you need to be happy with *you*.

Whatever obstacle you are now encountering in your life or your career is almost certainly going to put you in a position where you begin to question yourself. You may have lost some of your confidence, or you may feel empty without your significant other by your side. Maybe you are doubting your career path or questioning what it is that has brought you to this point. All of those reactions are perfectly understandable and perfectly normal for people who are enduring hardship.

But you know what? The events and circumstances changed, not you. You're the same person you were before this event occurred, and that person was confident, vibrant, and enthusiastic. Those are the very same qualities you will need in your bounce back. You are as strong as you ever were, and the sooner you see that, the better off you will be in recovering from this setback.

One thing I think back to a lot when my confidence is waning is the first time we were in New York City for a game with my UMass team. We were going to play in Madison Square Garden, and that was no small honor for me, a Pittsburgh kid who used to watch pro and college games on TV from MSG when I was young.

I was able to get my dad a room at the team hotel, and I'll never forget when I went to his room right after he had checked in. He shuttled me into the room like he had a secret; when I got inside, he closed the door and pointed to the hotel's rate card beneath the eye hole.

The maximum rate was highlighted, and it was something ridiculous—a typical exorbitant price in Manhattan, but not something Moon Township folks would often see. My dad just shook his head at me and said, "Son, keep doing what you're doing."

Think back to a moment when you felt that same kind of pride and accomplishment. It could be when you were able to take your family on an extravagant vacation, or a time when you closed a tough deal at work. You are still the person who was able to accomplish those things, and you will be able to achieve them again. Sudden change happens for all sorts of convoluted reasons, and often it's out of your hands. You could have been "downsized" for no other reason than the weak economy, or your marriage might have failed because of something your spouse did. Maybe you've done everything right, you've met every quota, and you've done all this for the company, but you were the low man on the totem pole, and they had to cut people loose.

Do you see what I'm getting at? You were talented and passionate enough to land the job in the first place or to find what you believed was true love. That part of you still exists, even if you can't quite feel it right now. Your job right now is to find out where those positive qualities reside within you and bring them to the surface. You are being asked to be your strongest during what could be one of your weakest moments, and that's not going to be easy. But it is going to be imperative for your recovery.

Relationship experts are fond of the expression that says, "You have to love yourself before you can love anyone else," and however trite you may find the words, it's the absolute truth. I'd even go as far as to say your bounce back can't be fully consummated without an acceptance of who you are and a realization that you deserve all the successes and joys that are going to come to you as you travel this road to renewal.

I promise not to get too spiritual on you over the course of this book—although I take my faith very seriously—but I've always believed that things have happened for a reason, even when that reason was not apparent immediately. Why would I ever have gone to Kansas to start my coaching career? I was an East Coast guy, not a Midwesterner. Well, you know what? Kansas is where I met my wonderful wife, Ellen. Or how about UMass? I mean, I almost took a job at the University of Maine before I settled on UMass. Why was that? Well, I don't fully know, but I do know my daughter Erin had the time of her life as a student at UMass, and I have to think that some of the reason I wound up in Amherst, Massachusetts, instead of Orono, Maine, was because it introduced Erin to what a tremendous campus and community UMass offers.

You have to know and accept that there is a bigger picture and life is bigger than you. Very likely, this pain and turmoil you're enduring now will wind up making you stronger, better, and more productive in your life and that of the community around you.

> **PractiCal Point:** Trust that good things will come from where you are now.

• • •

It would be neglectful of me as your coach if I didn't put in a few more minutes on this very important point of "getting right with yourself."

It's understandable if you are skeptical of your ability to find strength from within. But I'm going to share a story that was sent to me, and its origins trace back to a *Reader's Digest* article. It has taken on several variations over the years, but there is little doubt it's rooted in an actual event, and it vividly displays how powerful your mind and attitude can be.

The crux of the story goes like this: A man by the name of Nick was working his job in a rail yard during a midsummer day. Nick and his crewmates were allowed to knock off early in honor of their foreman's birthday. As Nick finished his work that day, he accidentally got locked in one of the yard's refrigerator boxcars. With everyone gone for the day, it's believed, Nick began to panic and frantically began banging and screaming for help.

But no one was around to hear Nick's desperate pleas. He apparently freaked out and began to focus on how cold he was and how little time he might have to live. He etched words into the boxcar's wooden floor. "It's so cold, my body is getting numb. . . . These may be my last words," he scrawled with a penknife.

The next morning, Nick's coworkers found his dead body in the refrigerated boxcar. They also found the refrigeration unit of the car had been inoperable for some time, and the thermometer inside read fifty-five degrees.

Nick didn't freeze to death; he worried himself to death. He made himself believe it was freezing and convinced himself he was dying.

Although the story is a parable, the message speaks to how powerful the human mind is. Our minds are strong enough to freeze us to death. Seriously. Think about that.

Imagine what the mind can do if your thoughts are optimistic and you attack your bounce back with a positive mental attitude. Believe me, I know that staying positive is easy to write about but a whole lot harder to do. You still need to make it a priority, every day from the minute you wake up to the minute you go to sleep.

I'd suggest you start by forcing out any negative thoughts that come into your mind. I've known people who have little sticky notes with STAY POSITIVE or TAKE CONTROL written on them and put the messages in strategic places: on mirrors, on the refrigerator, on the alarm clock, or on the car dashboard. I've heard of other people who keep uplifting messages on their desks or in their wallets. It can be almost anything, anywhere, as long it gets you thinking upbeat thoughts.

Career coach Bobbie LaPorte puts a great spin on how this phase of the bounce back can play out. She told me her most successful clients are the ones who quickly grasp the concept that whatever setback they have run into, it is now presenting an opportunity.

"When people start to come out of it and say, 'This is not a door closing; it's the next door opening,' they are starting off on the right foot," Bobbie told me. "I want people to look at it and think about how they will use this episode as a leverage point for themselves."

In other words, think about what you didn't like in the prior situation you were in. Maybe the atmosphere was negative, or you didn't feel appreciated for your contributions, or you weren't excited about what you did each day. Your situation right now is an opportunity to better those conditions in your career or life.

"There's always something in your situation that says, 'You know, I could do something different,'" Bobbie said. "Maybe you want something more challenging or more suitable to your best skill sets."

It's easy to forget the negative when you think about the past, especially if you feel like even a bad job or relationship is better than none at all. But this is your chance to put yourself in a better position. When you start seeing the benefits to the change you are dealing with, it becomes easier to envision a better situation ahead.

But if you prolong the act of getting past what has happened, you do two things and neither of them is good.

First, you allow the negative to dominate and become a self-fulfilling prophecy. If you think horrible thoughts, horrible results are sure to follow.

Second, and maybe more important, you are wasting time better spent planning your next series of moves. Use your energy for improving, not wallowing.

> **PractiCal Point:** Don't only recall the good, and realize there were also things that were less than ideal. From that you will appreciate the vast opportunities ahead of you.

. . .

There's no question you are currently dealing with a serious issue, and no one would be cruel enough to suggest it's not been a crushing blow for you. At the same time, though, as you're discovering, almost everything is resolvable in one manner or another.

One of the great things I came across while researching this book was a tip from Karen Salmansohn, a bestselling motivational author. In her smartly named 2007 book, *The Bounce Back Book,* Karen wrote:

> The only true observer of your world and your issues is YOU.
>
> During bad times, if you feel embarrassed by what others are thinking about you, fear not. Most people aren't thinking about all the things wrong in your world. They're *too* caught up with all the things wrong in their own worlds.

For a few weeks after I got fired by the Nets, Ellen and I would go out to dinner or be in a public setting, and I would think everyone was talking about me. The hair would stand up on the back of my neck, and I wanted to yell out, "WHAT? What did I do?" Ellen always kept me grounded though, saying, "John, they don't even know who you are. Eat your dinner."

She was so right, it was silly. You might go out to dinner in your town and think everyone in the restaurant is whispering about you and your situation. You become paranoid for no good reason. I was no different. I'd be having a nice meal with Ellen, and I'd become convinced the guy at the table near us was bad-mouthing me. He would invariably stop by the table and say, "They never should have fired you." He and others were just being supportive.. Crazy right? We tend to get so wrapped up in our own bounce back that we forget that almost everyone we come in contact with is going through his or her own individual bounce back or is involved in a loved one's difficult journey back to happiness.

Remember when I let you know in the letter at the start there would be tough love in this book? Well, here's one of those times, and it may not be what you want to hear right now. But it's what you need to hear. I'm being blunt because I care about my players, and I care about helping you through this difficult time.

IT'S ENOUGH ALREADY. YOU'VE WASTED ENOUGH TIME UNDER THOSE COVERS.

Get up, take a shower, walk the dog, and make this a pivotal day in the course of your bounce back.

You need to now push yourself to a place that might be uncomfortable. It may be a place you think you're not ready to visit or don't think you have the energy to get to. But this is what champions do— making themselves uncomfortable is the price of greatness, and at this time you need to go beyond your mind's and your body's flexibility.

Chances are you're feeling a bit queasy over the way things have been going. That uneasiness is common and explicable; it is not acceptable as a member of my team, and I know you have the ability to push past it.

You have to bust through your comfort zone and be the strongest even while you're feeling your weakest. Maybe you are suffering through very personal attacks and criticisms from people you may have thought were your allies. In my situation with the Nets, because it was so public, those slings and arrows were coming from more directions than I care to count. But what I had to do, and what you will need to do now, is master the ability to get past the pitfalls of emotionally overreacting. It's understandable if you're going through bouts of self-flagellation, angst, guilt, and regret. Accepting and acknowledging those emotions will hopefully convince you not to do anything rash or foolish.

You can foster those feelings for a very brief time, but you must avoid too many hours of wasted, negative, and unproductive energy. If you let the distress overcome you, I'm telling you it will keep you down and adversely affect everything we are trying to do in this book.

> **PractiCal Point:** Know that you are not the first, worst, or only. Others have been where you are and they're doing just fine now. But it took some time.

CHAPTER 4

NEXT!

THE POWER OF
AMNESIA

Let's take a time-out and look at where you are after three chapters of this book: You're out from under the covers now. You are optimistic and forward thinking. You've established a routine that gives you structure, and you have begun to create new habits that replace the old, destructive ones. Hopefully you've begun to laugh again and to feel more like yourself, projecting that persona to everyone you come in contact with.

Those are significant steps, and you need to take pride in having conquered them.

As a bit of a reward, here's where I'm going to cut my first deal with you as a member of my team. I don't do this often with my squads, but once in a while—especially if we're in a tough stretch of games—I will let the players know before a practice if they give 100 percent maximum effort in the next two hours and prove to me they are all clicking on the same cylinders, they will be rewarded with a day off.

For the next several pages, I will allow you to reflect and dissect the events that led up to your trigger event. I will even offer up some of the emotions I felt and lessons I was learning primarily after the Nets firing, but also after the Kansas loss. This will be the only portion of the book—and hopefully of your bounce back—where you are "allowed" to dwell a bit on the circumstances that have led to this point in your career or life.

The reason I am doing this is so I can coach you to a point of "closure" on the setback you have endured. That term gets thrown around a lot, especially for those who are grieving, but I fully believe it's important to work for and find closure on a difficult area of your life so that you can really move on. You really do need to get past the trigger event, the emotion, the anguish, and the regret so you can focus on your "next" life.

• • •

The standard mantras of the Calipari family when I grew up were "Rub some dirt in it" and "Grow up and get over it." It was a philosophy instilled in me and my two sisters (Lea and Terry) from my parents (Vince and Donna) and my grandparents. All of the adults in my life while I was growing up were very resilient people who had lived through the first Great Depression. My dad's family was on welfare when he was growing up. It always struck me how they never seemed to spend much time dwelling on the past. If you see an opportunity, swim like hell to grab it, was their philosophy. They taught my sisters and me not to wait for something good to happen, but instead to go and make sure it happens. I truly believe it is the responsibility of every parent to raise self-reliant kids who understand there will be ups, downs, and in-betweens.

However, the reality is you can't really move forward until you have taken stock of what happened. As unhealthy as dwelling on the past can be, ignoring it can be just as destructive.

Whatever your situation, now is the time when it's okay to reflect upon what has transpired. But you *cannot* become obsessed with the minutiae of what brought you to this point. I am allowing you this time to come to terms with the events of the past few weeks, months, or years in order for you to be able to move forward constructively and uninhibited.

Let me give you an example that goes back to our UMass days. This was in the mid-1990s when we had a point guard from Hartford, Connecticut, by the name of Mike Williams. Probably the best word to describe Mike was *mercurial*. But he was an unbelievably talented—and clutch—player. He was also an unbelievably frustrating player to coach. He was in and out of my dog house, and he tried my patience as much as any player I have ever coached.

Truth be told, I should have kicked him off the team two years before I did, but I thought I could be Father Flanagan and "save him." I was delusional. Whatever our team's upside was with him on the floor—and it was considerable—I could no longer tolerate Mike's immaturity and instability. Finally, in his senior year, in 1995, Mike screwed up for the last time, and I kicked him off the team. It was a gut-wrenching decision for me and my staff, but he had strayed over the line once too often.

The night before I made the announcement of his dismissal public, I was kissing my daughter Erin good night, and I felt like I should tell her what I was doing. She was only eight years old at the time, but Erin had grown close with all the players and was around the team a lot. I've always believed in bringing my players into my home as often as possible, and both Erin and Megan were like little sisters to many of our UMass players.

I looked at Erin that night and said, "I am throwing Mike Williams off the team."

Without blinking, she said, "Good!" and kissed me on the cheek, ready to head to bed. I was a bit stunned by her reaction because I knew she liked Mike and loved his ability to hit the big shot.

"Why is that good, honey?" I asked her.

"Because now maybe you won't talk about him so much anymore."

Once again, one of my children had put things in proper perspective for me. Good thing they take after their mom in that department!

I had become so obsessed with saving this young man that every phone call and every conversation I had was about Mike Williams. Even eight-year-old Erin had picked up on it, and she was absolutely right. I had become obsessed with Mike to the point of hurting the team. That's what overthinking your own bounce back situation can do to you. **If you become fixated on one aspect of the problem, you lose the ability to progress through the stages of your revitalization.**

Get the negative out of your psyche even if you think you're able to hide the pessimism. Most people you come in contact with will sense your bad vibes right away. Humans, by nature, can sense despair or anguish. Get rid of that baggage, and be as upbeat and positive as possible.

Before I take you through some of the ways I initially began to put the Nets behind me, let's be sure we're clear on one thing: if you're not honest about what has led you to where you are, then it's foolish to think your bounce back is going to have a chance of succeeding. You might want to point fingers and blame others at first, but you're wasting your time as a member of my team if that's the *only* thing you're going to do.

Listen, this part of your bounce back isn't going to be easy, and it's

62

also not going to be the final time that you look back at the developments that led you here. But for our purposes it needs to be the period of time that you are most willing to openly and candidly assess how you arrived at this point. It's hard to take responsibility, but it's harder to move on unless you do.

I look at it this way: the Nets moved on, installed a new coach, and played out the schedule. They were "over" me very quickly. I had to stop viewing myself as a victim or worrying that I was being targeted by them. There were millions before me, and there will be millions after me who will deal with some kind of devastation in their lives. Feeling sorry for myself wasn't going to help anyone, least of all myself and my family. This was no time to let emotion get in the way of clear, forward thinking. Ralph Waldo Emerson put it this way, "For every minute you are angry, you lose sixty seconds of happiness."

My dad always used to say an accountant shouldn't make a career move in April—during tax time he is not able to think rationally in the thick of his busiest season. Likewise, I always say a basketball coach shouldn't make a decision within two weeks of the season ending because he hates everything, having just gone through the grind of all those games and practices and meetings. The feelings are too raw and too irrational in the immediate aftermath for anyone to be able to think lucidly. You need to allow some time to pass before you can begin the closure process; hopefully that time is now.

Here's a great quote I read in a *Fortune* magazine article from June 2008. It comes from Mickey Drexler, the former CEO of Gap, Inc., the clothing giant. When he was fired in 2002, Mickey said, "I was angry. I cried. But getting fired was one of the best things that could have happened to me. It taught me about opening too many stores and made me a better operator," as the CEO of J.Crew, where

Mickey wound up and wouldn't "dare let overexpansion hamper growth profit."

The lesson you should take out of Mickey's quote is that no matter how terrible you feel your situation is at the moment, you can learn from your mistakes and become a better person for them.

> **PractiCal Point:** Prepare yourself for an honest self-evaluation and serious introspection.

· · ·

As you read over the next few pages, I want to you focus on a couple of key points. Understand that as I write this, I have the benefit of a decade's having passed since I was fired by the New Jersey Nets. In the days and weeks after the trigger event takes place, you might not be able to see things as clearly as you will a year, five years, or a decade later. That doesn't mean you aren't able to fairly assess what you have been through; it's just a warning that the further removed you are from your setback, the more you will be able to accurately appraise the chain of events you experienced. I was able to honestly assess what had happened with the Nets after a few weeks had gone by, but with each passing year I continue to learn and grow when I consider aspects that I hadn't originally thought about.

Whether or not I was able to see it in 1999 or in 2009, the most valuable benefit of my bounce back was the ability to compartmentalize things that happened in the past and move forward onto the next step of my bounce back. It's that very powerful four letter word—**Next**—that I want you to focus on right now.

Come to any of my practices, and chances are you will hear me yell, "NEXT!" During our 2007–08 Final Four season, I must have said that word more times than a counter worker at the Department of Motor Vehicles.

If Chris Douglas-Roberts missed a shot, I'd scream it. "NEXT!" If Derrick Rose caused a turnover, I'd holler: "NEXT!" Whenever there was a miscue or an unwanted result, my immediate response was always "NEXT!"

Over time, each of the players who come into our basketball family understands what I mean when I scream the word. Everyone understands we're moving on to the next play instead of harping on the prior one. It's a trick that all star players have had to master; they know that one (or two or three) mistakes can happen, but they also know that they have to keep pushing forward in order to keep their edge. I have so much respect for what Jamie Dixon has done with the Pittsburgh program, and this story from the 2008–09 season (when the Panthers advanced to the Elite 8) in particular caught my eye:

Battling No. 1–in-the-nation UConn in a key late-season Big East game in Hartford, Connecticut, Pitt was tied with the Huskies, 61–61. Levance Fields had struggled all game and found himself in a 0 of eight shooting slump. With 3:09 left, Levance buried a 3-pointer for his first points of the game. Less than a minute later he nailed another 3-ball to give the Panthers a six-point lead. He wound up scoring all ten of his points in the final 3:09 as Pitt knocked off UConn and ascended to the No. 1 ranking for the second time in school history.

After the game, Levance told reporters: "I think every shot I take is going in so it didn't matter how many I had missed," he said. "It didn't matter that I missed the first eight, I got the biggest two."

I thought to myself, that's exactly why Levance is going to have a long career at the next level. He wasn't fazed by his eight misses; he barely even acknowledged them. Instead he constantly thought about making his next shot.

Learn from that. **If you're constantly looking back at your failures, you're limiting your future successes.** This is why it's so important to get right with yourself and find the love you had for yourself when things were going well. When you have that confidence in yourself, the fear—and thus the failure—cannot live.

You have to do everything in your power to objectively assess what it is that has led you to this particular point. I wasn't able to do it right away because the bitterness and venom I was feeling was still percolating inside me.

But the further away I was able to get from the situation, the more truthful I could be with myself. I want to urge you to get beyond the anger as quickly as possible. To do that, you need to be willing to accept responsibility even if you can't fully process all that has happened. **Your failures are not nearly as deep or as damaging as you think they are.**

Maybe the best example of this concept of "Next" is my former point guard, Sammy Cassell. Sammy has had a fifteen-year career in the NBA, playing for eight different teams, and he has three NBA championship rings to show for it, including one with the Boston Celtics in 2007–08. Sammy is a winner, and we have always gotten along great, going back to his days as a college player at Florida State when I was at UMass. To watch us during our time together in New Jersey, many people might have thought we were constantly at war, but nothing could have been further from the truth. Did we battle and squabble? Sure. But we did that because we both had one goal in mind: winning.

There would be times during games when I would tell Sammy to pass more, and he would come over to the sideline and say, "Coach, do you want me to pass or do you want us to win?" That's Sammy—he was never being cocky, but he was always confident—he has swagger.

During our 2007–08 Final Four season at Memphis, I brought in Sammy to talk to my team about the need to have amnesia on the basketball court. That need is as important on the parquet as it is in your bounce back. If you miss a shot, forget about it. If you turn the ball over, forget about it. Sammy was the absolute best at that. He could miss ten shots in a row, but he absolutely believed that next shot was going in. It's what has made him one of the deadliest and most clutch shooters in the NBA, and it has helped him to extend his NBA career over parts of two decades.

"If you dwell on something like a missed shot or a turnover, it's going to affect how you attack the next possession," Sammy told my team. "You can't control what happened on the last play. It's over. Whatever happened—good or bad—is done. You need to refocus on what you're going to do the next time you touch the ball. The other way, it will [mess] with your mind. *All* guys in the NBA go through slumps. Everyone. But it's how fast you are able to forget the slump and forget what has happened that will separate the good from the great. You cannot dwell on what has happened."

That's what Sammy is all about, and he even told me it has carried over into his everyday life. "If I make a bad decision with my money, I have to accept it and move on," he told me in December 2008. "If you dwell on the bad investment or the poor decision, it will drive you crazy, Cal. I've made some bad investments—we all have—but I haven't let that prevent me from other deals. Without risk, there's no reward."

I couldn't agree more. Let me tell you something else: the minute

I was able to admit that I failed on some levels with the Nets was the minute my bounce back truly started to take shape. It was very difficult at first because we had gone to the playoffs the year before, and even though we were swept in three games by Michael Jordan and the Chicago Bulls, our playoff berth was viewed around the league as a positive step in the right direction. I knew I had done great work and didn't think I should be punished for it.

But let's face it; I wasn't perfect with the Nets. I made mistakes at every level of my job description.

They were issues that stemmed from my own inexperience, and I can tell you for sure that I would handle each of them differently now. That's all part of getting older and wiser and figuring out how to deal with people. While regrettable, these examples were not fatal; I'm confident that your past transgressions aren't either.

It's imperative for you to realize that you cannot blame others for where you now find yourself. Take responsibility, learn from the errors of your way, and move forward. This is not an option; it's a demand if you're going to remain on my team. No matter how hard it might be, it's critically important to own up to your own shortcomings; you have to be able to recognize your weaknesses before you can overcome them.

In most businesses and many circumstances, no one wants to hear your problems. In the NBA especially, it's about winning. Just look at the first quarter of the 2008–09 NBA season: by the time Christmas rolled around, six of the league's thirty coaches had been fired. Twenty percent! It wasn't personal; that league is about results and results only. Plain and simple, I got fired in New Jersey because we started off with a 3–17 record.

It's fine to look back and assess what you would have done differently. I even asked Jim Donald, the ex-CEO of Starbucks and a friend from my days in New Jersey, what he would have done differently during his run with the retail coffee giant. About three months after he was let go, he didn't hesitate with his explanation.

"My worst decision, Cal, was not investing earlier in international," Jim told me. "The international markets don't have as quick returns as the United States', but if I had known the U.S. economy was going to crash, I would have invested earlier."

Jim was able to reasonably assess his shortcoming, and doing that made it easier for him to move on. It took him some time to be able to do it, but it made his transition into his next opportunities all the more easy.

Would I have been able to admit all those things I wrote above during the first few weeks after the Nets fired me? Maybe not. But the weeks, months, and years since have allowed me to reflect on all aspects of the experience.

That's exactly what the Nets job was for me—an experience. It was one chapter in the book of my life, and that's exactly what your current situation is. Even if you are not able to see it clearly now, you have to understand that, as the saying goes, "this, too, shall pass." This process of truthful evaluation will aid you in reaching that level of strength and confidence you need.

Now, for the sake of contrast, let me give you an example of someone who was not ready to accept his failings, and because of it, he hampered the progress of his bounce back.

I'm not going to use this coach's name because he's a good friend, a great leader, and a really caring and considerate guy. In 2008, the coach was fired from his job as a sub–Division I head coach after having been there for quite a few years.

He seemed to know it was coming, but he couldn't stop it. Shortly after the axe fell, he called me and asked for some advice and guidance.

"Let me ask you this," I said to him in one of our talks. "How did you leave things with your athletic director and the administrators?"

"I'm okay with the AD," he said. "But I didn't get along too well with the president and a few of his underlings. They're the ones who really wanted to see me go."

I could hear from the tone of his voice he had a lot of bitterness and anger raging inside.

"Well, what are you going to do to mend fences with those people?" I asked.

"Mend fences, Cal?" he asked. "Why would I do that? I'm never going to work for those people again."

"Maybe, maybe not. But you are going to work in college basketball again, right?"

"Yeah, that's one of the reasons I'm calling you. I was hoping you could put some feelers out."

"I'm happy to do that for you," I said. "But before I can do that, you have to go back and talk to those people you say had it out for you, and you need to reconcile with them. Being 'good' with the AD isn't enough. Not only do ADs speak to ADs when they're looking to hire coaches, but presidents talk to presidents, provosts talk to provosts—everyone on a campus has his own circle he runs in, and it's those people he leans on when he's doing background on a potential hire."

My friend wasn't real happy with that response, but he said he understood and would try his best to smooth things over.

But I knew after talking to him, he wasn't yet ready to look back and accept his mistakes and missteps. He just wasn't at that point yet, and there was no amount of help I could offer to him until he was.

I truly believe being able to assess what you have been through and then being able to neatly tuck that assessment away in a box will be one of the most important early stages of your comeback. By doing this, you will be able to move forward with less baggage and a clearer focus.

> **PractiCal Point:** Assess your past situation objectively and honestly, and be willing to mend fences.

. . .

Okay, per the deal I made with you at the beginning of this chapter, you have now reached the stage of your bounce back where dwelling on, ruing, or ruminating over past occurrences is no longer acceptable. Will this be an easy transition for you to make? No, but I never promised this was going to be a breeze. At the most, for the next week or so of your bounce back, I will allow you to take five to ten minutes a day to think about past "failures"; psychologists generally agree that allowing the rumination to take place for a definitive amount of time does offer relief, but once you reach that time limit, it's time to focus on your next moves. Remember what Sammy Cassell told my Tigers: "If you dwell on something like a missed shot or a turnover, it's going to affect how you attack the next possession."

PRACTICE PLAN #2

HOW DID I GET HERE?

EMPHASIS OF THE DAY: Discovering what led you to where you are now

There is no looking forward until you have looked back, and this practice plan will help you organize your thoughts on the series of events and moments that led you to this point in your life.

Before your trigger event happened, there was a host of circumstances—both positive and negative—that unfolded and resulted in your crisis. Understanding these situations and honestly evaluating and dissecting them will be hugely beneficial in the coming days, weeks, and months. You will be able to look back on the origins of your current predicament and ensure that you won't make the same mistakes again.

PURPOSE

In addition to providing a list of Don'ts, this exercise will inevitably show you there were things that led to your trigger event that were completely out of your control.

When I was a young coach in my first years at UMass, I was too concerned with what others were saying or writing about me. I wasted a lot of energy on trying to get "my side" of the story into the public domain. Now, I realize that it just doesn't matter what others are saying about me because I can't control those things.

Once you have completed this drill, you will hopefully be able to acknowledge both the mistakes you made and the accomplishments you achieved. It's never as bad as it seems.

DRILL

Be honest with yourself, and don't be afraid to include things that weren't entirely your fault or ones you are still trying to resolve in your head. The more specific you can be, the better, so when you look back on this drill, you will be able to quickly identify patterns that were harmful in the past.

You need to think big picture here and not get bogged down in the little things. For instance, if you're going through a separation or divorce, don't kill yourself over idiosyncrasies or pet peeves you or your spouse may have had. The fact that you didn't install the toilet paper in the "under" way instead of the "over" way is not what led to your estrangement (if it is, you need more help than this book can offer!).

Concentrate on the major conflicts or issues that truly affected your situation. I turn again to something NFL player Junior Seau said, "Major in the major and minor in the minor."

WATCH ME FIRST

* *I spent too little time focusing on my team and too much time concentrating on the next opponent. I learned from Coach Brown that in the NBA you are better off worrying about your own team than wasting time on what the other team may or may not do.*
* *I'm an emotional Italian—always have been and always will be. Some people made a point about my passion during games,*

and they were right. At times I was too loud, and I probably coached too much during games. My sideline demeanor was a bit too rambunctious. It was what I knew and what worked for me in college, but some NBA players would not respond to that type of coaching.

- *When the Nets were sold to a new ownership group led by Ray Chambers, Finn Wentworth, and Lewis Katz in 1998, I didn't do enough to foster the communal relationship I had with the previous owners. (The owners who hired me were known as the "Secaucus Seven" and consisted of Henry and Joe Taub, Alan Aufzien, David Gerstein, Jerry Cohen, Bernie Mann, and Don Unger.) To this day, I still talk with Joe and David, and I have a great relationship with Brett Yormark, the current president and CEO of Nets Sports and Entertainment. But I didn't build that level of trust with the new owners. Overall, that was probably my biggest failure. I was so focused on coming out of the lockout with a viable team that I neglected to make time for getting to know the new group of owners.*

- *I antagonized the media—way too far in one instance—and wound up embarrassing myself and the organization in the process. In the New York media market you just can't get on the press's bad side or they will crucify you; I learned the hard way that no matter how frustrated I was feeling or however funny I was trying to be, I had to always be thinking about my reputation and my role as a representative for my organization.*

- *I should have fought harder to keep Sammy Cassell. Ultimately I approved of the Stephon Marbury trade, but if I had listened to my gut, I would have opposed it more vehemently. Likewise, I would have done everything in my power to trade*

Jayson Williams. Heck, I would have traded him for a mascot. Bill Parcells once told me during one of my visits to watch his Jets team practice that if the biggest personality on your team is not the guy you want, you better do everything in your power to get rid of him. "Because," Bill told me, "he's sure as heck trying to get rid of you." And, as usual, "The Tuna" was right.

CHAPTER 5

DISCOVER YOUR OWN BEST VERSION

WHAT WILL YOUR BOUNCE BACK BE MADE UP OF?

Let's now work a little bit on shaping what it is you are hoping to gain from your bounce-back journey. In other words, how are we going to Define Your Success? Will it be strictly a monetary definition of success? Will it have to do with where you are living or whom you are living with? Will your success be dependent on someone else, or are you prepared to determine your own triumph?

During the 2008–09 season I read a powerful book from the bestselling author Matthew Kelly, titled *The Rhythm of Life: Living Every Day with Passion and Purpose*. It was a really inspirational read; one of the greatest things Kelly discussed in the book was his focus on creating the best possible "version of you."

That struck me immediately, and I brought it to my Memphis team the day after I read it in early January 2009. I asked the players on the team if they were living the best version of their lives. "Are you doing everything to your utmost in every facet of your lives?" I asked them.

We went around the locker room and everyone—players and

coaches—answered "no." Some guys said they weren't eating the right foods. Others said they weren't doing enough individual work. Still others were disappointed in the way they were treating their families or friends. I even chimed in and admitted I wasn't happy with the physical shape I was in and wanted to work out more (I wound up dropping twenty-five pounds from mid-November to the end of the season).

It was a very revealing conversation, and it certainly got the attention of my team. "If you're not doing the best you can in everything you do, then you're not living the best-version-of-yourself," I said. "That's awfully wasteful, and it is no way to go through a season, a year, or a life. Every day, you have to be making decisions that will help you be the best person you can be."

It's a conversation I now want to have with you. Are you living the best-version-of-yourself you possibly can?

In order to answer "yes" to that question, you have to be able to look at yourself in the mirror and say, without hesitation, you are treating others fairly. You need to be able to acknowledge that not everything that has happened in your life has been foisted upon you. What I mean by that is you need to be taking responsibility for past transgressions, and you have to make sure you will not resort to placing blame for situations you were or will be in.

The-best-version-of-yourself, according to Matthew Kelly, involves your "[taking] time each day to visualize that person you are capable of becoming. If you cannot visualize the better person you wish to become, you cannot become that better person. . . . Visualize particular ways of acting in certain situations. . . .

"All great change," Kelly writes, "is first an idea in our minds. The first expression of every great achievement in history has been in the wonder of the imagination. Visualize the changes you wish to achieve."

That's some powerful stuff, isn't it?

It's also in line with something I tell my players and reinforce throughout any given season. I want every individual on my team to own his performance. That means when a young man is playing poorly and he's shooting poorly and he's playing timidly, he has to own it and say, "I am not performing to my best ability." All too often, human nature tells us to only own our good performances and our triumphs. But in order to be true to yourself, you need to own *everything* you do—good and bad. I've had players complain, "Coach takes me out [of the game] every time I make a mistake." A lot of times it's true, but the reason I do it is to prevent those mistakes from becoming habits. People who are willing to own their performance will get this. Players who don't do so get buried on the bench.

If you are struggling, you have to change what you are doing and not let it overtake you. How do you do that? You spend extra time and work on yourself. For my guys, that means getting to the gym early and staying late. It means asking for help. It means taking control and, as Kelly said, making the best possible version of you.

Understand this: confidence is demonstrated performance. That's how you build confidence—you show you are poised and self-confident. In basketball, what it means is that you go on the court and demonstrate you can *really* play, and as you do, you build your own confidence. In life you attack every day with gusto so that with each step forward you build assuredness into the very soul of your being. From there, you create what Kelly would term the best-version-of-yourself.

When I was a young coach just making my way up the ladder,

I think I put a lot of weight on making money, winning championships, and putting players in the NBA. As I've gotten older and wiser, my priorities have changed, and along with that, my definition of success has also been altered. I now base my success on less material things—not that I don't enjoy the finer things in life.

But I measure my success now on how many lives I've been able to affect in a positive way. It's not just the lives of my players I'm talking about. I want to be having an impact on my assistants, on other people in the athletic department, and on people within the community.

With that as my definition, I have made a dedicated effort to not only be the best coach I can be, but to be the best husband, father, son, brother, uncle, and community leader I can be. I'm constantly focusing on how I treat people and making sure the way I interact with others is the same way I would want them to interact with me. It's the old Golden Rule of "Do unto others as you would have them do unto you," one of life's most enduring truisms. Treating people the way you want to be treated is a time-honored tradition. If you have a caring heart, you will be compassionate in your dealings with others and be amazed at what you get back from them.

I truly believe—and hope—this book will be a lasting legacy of how my success is defined not only by others, but by me. I want this book to have an impact on everyone who reads it, and I want our community of bounce backers (at **www.coachcalbounceback.com**) to then have an impact on others.

When you are coming up with your own definition of personal success, I want you to keep in mind the importance of ensuring that success is not solely inward based. Think about how your own success can positively impact on those around you, and make that a priority as you enter this next stage of your bounce back.

> **PractiCal Point:** Determine what the best-version-of-yourself should look like, and show it to everybody.

· · ·

Another insightful observation from Matthew Kelly in his book that caught my eye was this one:

> Knowing who we are (strengths, weaknesses, needs, talents, and desires) and what we are here for (to become the-best-version-of-ourselves) is the knowledge that liberates us from the modern enslavement of a life of meaninglessness and gives our lives back to us once more.

To me, what Kelly is saying here is similar to what I do with every team I coach. I'd be a fool to try and coach every team the exact same way. Some teams—like my Final Four teams at Memphis and UMass—were led by seniors who had been with me and knew exactly what it was we were trying to accomplish and how we'd get there. During our 2008 Final Four run at Memphis, I had friends and other coaches coming up to me and marveling at how little coaching it appeared I was doing on the sideline.

"When you've got Superman [Derrick Rose] at the point," I'd tell them, "you might as well sit back and enjoy the show."

I was still very much in control of that team, but at the same time I was confident enough in my upperclassmen that I could empower them to handle things on the court for the vast majority of the game.

That all changed with the 2008–09 edition of the Tigers, as we had several new pieces we were working into the rotation.

I was doing a lot of screaming and yelling during games. I was jumping up and down, yelling, hollering, cajoling—I did just about everything except go on the court and grab a rebound! But that was what my young team needed from me. Superman wasn't at the point anymore, and everyone was still adapting to their roles.

But that's fine. Because I knew they would need to be coached more aggressively, I prepared myself for what it would entail.

For your bounce back, you're going to have to realize that what you've done in the past might not always work for you now. **You have to be adaptable;** you will do that by having a positive attitude, unrivaled energy, and vision of where you are headed. Hopefully by now you have been able to establish a regular routine for yourself and have also been able to start formulating what your plan of attack will be to move your bounce back into high gear.

Matthew Kelly calls this process "the journey of the soul," and asks readers to envision going from Point A, the person you are today, to Point B, the-best-version-of-yourself. He writes:

> Point A represents you . . . right now—here and today—with all your strengths and weaknesses, faults, failings, flaws, defects, talents, abilities, and potential.
>
> Point B represents you as the person you were created to be—perfectly. If you close your eyes for a few moments and imagine the better person you know you can be in any area of your life, and then multiply that vision to include the better person you know you can be in every area of your life, that is the person you have become when you reach Point B—the-best-version-of-yourself. . . .
>
> Dedicate yourself above all else to becoming the-best-version-of-yourself. It is the best thing you can do for your

spouse, your children, your friends, your colleagues, your employees, your employer, your church, your nation, the human family, and yourself. The best thing you can do is to become the-best-version-of-yourself, because it is *doing* with a *purpose*.

Embrace your essential purpose. Celebrate your best self.

Once you are able to this, you are going to be able to see things much clearer as they relate to your bounce back. You don't want to be undertaking this process as a flawed human being because you will end up with a flawed result. You have to recognize that success won't come from doing the same things you've always done. It will come from your ability to adapt to your new situation, even if it means using a different skill set or a different definition of yourself than what you had before. You have to be willing to see—and be— the best-version-of-yourself in order to define your own success.

> **PractiCal Point:** Work to reaching a point where you are empowered by your confidence, positive attitude, and flexibility.

• • •

This process of defining your own success is going to lead quite naturally into a clear and definitive game plan for how you want to move forward in your bounce back. That plan is going to be strategically important when you begin to reach out to others for help in your recovery, because you want to be sure that you are clear and certain about what it is you want to do and how you want your contacts to help you.

I took a lot of time during this stage of my bounce back to carefully consider what it was that not only made me happiest in life, but what fulfilled the lives of Ellen and the kids the most. I had a pretty good inkling that I would stay in coaching, but it wasn't as definite as you may think.

I remember at first telling Ellen that maybe I would just be a stay-at-home dad. I could do some side scouting work or maybe some television, and I would be able to watch my children grow up. That really did appeal to me. But Ellen was having none of that. Early on, she put the kibosh on those thoughts. "No way," she said smiling, the way only my wife can, "you'll drive us all crazy."

Once I got those thoughts out of my head, I started to think about what it was that interested me the most, and I kept coming back to the game of basketball I had loved so much since my early days as a gym rat in Moon Township. Sure, I had just been dumped by the one I loved, but the Nets weren't the only team in the world. Ultimately, I knew I wanted to get back into coaching, and I was pretty sure I wanted it to be at the college level. But before I would be able to get another coaching job, I also wanted to experience a little more of the TV work I had enjoyed during my time at UMass. I had my own TV show and radio show in Amherst, and my friends at ESPN in Bristol would often bring me into their studios to offer commentary on college games. It was an ego boost for sure, and after the Nets firing, I needed a little infusion of ego.

So I started with that on my list of what I wanted to do over the next six, twelve, or eighteen months. I still had some connections at the networks, so I was fairly confident I could land a part-time TV job.

I knew that would only be a temporary thing and I had to focus more on what I was going to do long-term. It was about this time when I started—quite naturally, I am now told—to have more pronounced anxiety and fear about what exactly I would be doing in the next year.

I'm fairly certain you may be experiencing some of that same fearfulness. Here's what I would tell you on that:

The fear of failure can paralyze even the strongest of us, and when you are in a vulnerable position like the one you may now be experiencing, that fear can be even more debilitating. To counter those emotions, you should always ask yourself, *What's the worst thing that can happen if I take this path?* I'm telling you that 99 percent of the time, that outcome is going to be something quite palatable, but the fear is going to make it seem unworthy.

That's where perseverance comes into play.

> **PractiCal Point:** Think long and hard about what it is you want to do next and then what you want to do after that.

• • •

Let me share a story of perseverance with you that I was able to witness firsthand. Not only is this a tale about resolve, it's also an example of how to overcome obstacles in a way that positions you for the next opportunity.

My dad, Vince, grew up outside Pittsburgh in the time of the Great Depression. Like a lot of his friends, he went to work in the local steel mills when he was a teenager. Neither he nor my mom, Donna, were college educated, but like my pal Dick Vitale says of his parents, my folks had a "PhD in love." They saved just about every penny they made so they could give me and my two sisters the best lives possible.

Around the time my dad was twenty years old, his buddies convinced him that there was better money to be made fueling airplanes at Pittsburgh International Airport. He was hesitant at first because the steel mills were all he knew. But he relented and took a chance.

He hooked on with Allied Aviation, a company that provided fuel for all the planes that came through Pittsburgh. Eventually, the airlines figured out it would be cheaper if they could fuel their own planes and not have an outside party like Allied doing the work. My dad had been with the company for twenty-plus years, and, boom, one day they announced they were going out of business. The only "compensation" was they would rehire the laid-off employees as hourly workers at something like five bucks an hour without any benefits.

So here he was at age fiftysomething with no job. My sisters and I were out of the house already, in college, but there was no way my dad could just stop working.

I wasn't living at home at the time Allied went out of business, but I was very aware of what my dad was going through. I'd call home and talk to him and my mom, and I knew they were struggling with what my dad's next move should be. Was it time to change careers? He was fifty and hadn't known any other job for twenty-plus years. Would they have to move? My family had been in the Pittsburgh area for generations, and neither my mom nor dad could imagine living anywhere else (they did eventually move to Charlotte, North Carolina, where they live today).

My dad was wrestling with some of the very same issues you may be facing right now. He had priorities—my mom, our family—and had deep ties to the area where he lived. I learned so much by watching him go through that situation. He made the decision that he would try and go part-time for a while with Piedmont and see where that led. It wasn't ideal, but it was what he and my mom determined would be the best thing for both of them. He had enough determination and enough trust in his abilities that everything would work out. When it all played out, his leap of faith paid off. After a year or so as a part-timer, he was hired full-time with benefits. Piedmont wound up being bought out by USAir, and my dad stayed with them until his retirement a few years ago at the age of seventy.

But that would never have been the case if he hadn't persevered through the shock and turmoil of Allied's going out of business. He believed in himself enough and knew he was strong enough and resilient enough to get through the rough patch. My dad always had a saying: **"Think it, talk it, it will happen."**

That's exactly what I did during my third and final year at Pitt. I started to really think seriously about what my future in the business of basketball would be. Almost every day when I was at Pitt, I would go for a run around campus. Running has always been a great way for me to both release some tension and gather my thoughts.

During those runs at Pitt, I created a scenario where I was the head coach of a basketball program, and each day I would go through—in my mind—what I would be doing that day if I had my own program.

Now, I didn't just make up some imaginary program; instead I picked a school that I knew a little something about and one about which I'd be able to legitimately simulate all aspects of running my own program.

The school I chose was Canisius College in Buffalo. I think I picked Canisius because, as a high schooler, I had played on an all-star team organized and coached by Irv Saracki, a teacher from the Buffalo area. We practiced in a gym on the Canisius campus, so I was familiar with the school's facilities, its location, and its potential.

(A few names you may recognize from that all-star team were future NBA draftees Mike Helms and Jim Johnstone, who both played at Wake Forest, and Rob Gonzalez, who played with Magic Johnson on the legendary 1979 national champion Michigan State Spartans before transferring to Colorado.)

Canisius was (and is) what we now call a midmajor program. It would be just the type of a job a first-time head coach would take to start his career. (In fact, my former assistant Chuck Martin is getting his start in Canisius's league, the MAAC.)

I started out on my runs in the off-season, and I would literally go through every facet of what it would entail to run that program. On my first few runs, I started with whom I would hire for my staff. I knew I would want experienced assistants who were young, aggressive go-getters unafraid to battle in the recruiting trenches. I wanted staff members who were familiar with the league and the region we would be recruiting in, which for Canisius would be mostly in New York State and the northeast. Other days I would move on to scheduling and then what my recruiting approach would be.

Then, for a week straight as I ran, I plotted what teams we could schedule as nonconference opponents before getting into the slate of what was then the North Atlantic Conference (now the Metro Atlantic Athletic Conference). I made it a mix of teams we would have a good shot at beating and teams that would challenge us and prepare us for the conference games. I literally had a list of ten schools I wanted to "schedule" for my "first season" as the Canisius head coach. From there, during my runs, I would formulate how we would recruit and what areas of New York we would focus on.

Each and every day during my run, I'd envision different scenarios that I would encounter once I had my own program. What style of basketball would we play? What would our uniforms look like?

Where would our logo be placed on our home floor? How could I help with fund-raising? What was the best outlet to have my coach's show on both radio and television?

I even went as far as to start picking out furniture for our basketball offices!

I look back on those runs now and laugh for a couple of reasons. First, it really did make my runs go by faster, so in that sense it was a great distraction for me. But second, it gave me some concrete goals to strive for as I began my quest to land a head job. Those goals, almost by definition, were positive thoughts constantly driving me in everything I was doing during my time at Pitt. I never let the planning interfere with my responsibilities for Coach Evans, but at the same time I used those sessions to constantly expand on what I was learning every day *with* Coach Evans.

This is exactly the type of exercise I want you to be doing at this stage of your bounce back. If you're hoping to reconcile with your significant other, I want you to be thinking of ways you can make your relationship strong and healthy. If you're going to be changing professions, you should be game-planning for what it is you want to do and how your skill set will fit the new job. If you're trying to get out of debt, you need to be thinking of prudent ways to save money and what the essential things you will allow yourself to spend money on.

PractiCal Point: Get specific and detailed about how you will capitalize on the reentry opportunity you will receive.

PRACTICE PLAN #3

CREATE A PERSONAL INVENTORY

EMPHASIS OF THE DAY: Create your "Sweet 16 " personal inventory.

By candidly assessing your own mental, ethical, and moral makeup, this drill will serve as the outline for my forthcoming request of you to "Write Your Own Story." The list below is something I adapted for my team members from a "Personal Inventory" worksheet that career coach Bobbie LaPorte directed my attention toward. There are several variations, and you are welcome to search the internet for one you feel caters better to your specific bounce back.

The personal inventory is a bit more of a broad outline of your strengths and weaknesses and certainly will be more useful for those of you going through a career-based bounce back. That's not to say it won't be beneficial for everyone, but it may take some tinkering to have it fit your particular situation.

PURPOSE

By making an effort to provide honest and introspective answers, these Sweet 16 questions will give a broad overview of what it is you are striving for during your bounce back and what will ultimately constitute a successful journey from your trigger event all the way through to your reentry opportunity. Once you are done, I want you to put your responses in order of importance, and be sure you are comfortable with the inventory you have taken.

One caution before you attack this assignment with the passion and concentration you must display with everything we work on: do not fall victim to what I call "analysis to paralysis." It is fine to spend considerable time with this questionnaire and contemplate it for a while, but don't let it overwhelm you. The answers you give are very important, but this will not be the final time in your bounce back where you are able to consider what form your ultimate success will take. In fact, as we move forward, some of your vision may change, and some of your priorities may need rearranging. Your bounce back is a living, breathing entity, and it needs to be fed, watered, and nurtured. These Sweet 16 replies you provide are the initial sustenance for your rebirth but are by no means the only sustenance.

DRILL

CAL'S SWEET 16 PERSONAL
INVENTORY QUESTIONS

(Provide answers to these sixteen prompts, and then arrange them in order of most important to least important.)

1. The top priorities in my career and life are:

2. I am very proud of:

3. I am most effective when:

4. I am least effective when:

5. If I could be anything I wanted professionally, I'd be:

6. I am most creative when:

7.   The most difficult business/personal decision I have ever made was:

8.   I would say that my greatest uniqueness is:

9.   I feel happiest when:

10. I feel lowest when:

11. What I like best about myself is:

12. What I like least about myself is:

13. The most important lesson I have learned in my life is:

14. To me, security is:

15. To me, money is:

16. In order to succeed, I need to:

WATCH ME FIRST

*COACH CAL'S RESPONSES TO THE
SWEET 16 PERSONAL INVENTORY QUESTIONS*

(As of April 2009)

1.   The top priorities in my career and life are: helping as many players and staff members as possible achieve their goals.

2.   I am very proud of: the graduation rates my programs at UMass and Memphis had.

3.   I am most effective when: things are swirling and there seems to be chaos or crisis.

4.   I am least effective when: things are going too well and my swagger becomes arrogance.

5.   If I could be anything I wanted professionally, I'd be: some type of career coach—something I've discovered through the writing of this book.

6.   I am most creative when: people are throwing ideas at me.

7.   The most difficult business/personal decision I have ever made was: accepting the Kentucky job—because it was so hard to leave Memphis.

8.   I would say my greatest uniqueness is: my ability to motivate.

9.   I feel happiest when: collectively we're achieving goals and people around me are benefiting from that success.

10. I feel lowest when: I'm having no impact on or not connecting with a player.

*11. What I like best about myself is: when I focus on something, **nothing** can impede my progress toward that goal.*

12. What I like least about myself is: when I become obsessed with accomplishing something to the point it takes me away from being a good father and husband.

13. The most important lesson I have learned in my life is: surround yourself with good people.

14. To me, security is: the comfort of knowing I have special friends and family who support me.

15. To me, money is: a way to reach out and help causes or people I want to help and to be able to do it without a second thought. I was fine financially after the Nets fired me, so everything else is now about helping others.

16. In order to succeed, I need to: constantly see that if you help people get what they want, you'll always have what you want.

CHAPTER 6

VISUALIZE YOUR SUCCESS

BE RELENTLESSLY POSITIVE, AND BELIEVE IN YOURSELF

I've always had a vivid imagination, ever since I was a little kid. Most of the time my dreams were sports related, and I'd find myself in game-deciding situations either hitting a last-second game winner in basketball or throwing a touchdown on the final play of the game, the way one of my heroes, Fran Tarkenton, used to.

As I got into my late-elementary-school days, I channeled those dreams into countless hours in the backyard or even just sitting in a hallway inside our house. I used to roll up a couple of socks and take shot after shot into the curtain rods hanging from my parents' windows. It seems silly now, but I'd spend hours creating all types of scenarios for "my team" as I drained jumpers and stuffed dunks. What did you want from me? I didn't have a brother, so I had to make my own fun sometimes.

When I'd get in the backyard—or out to the tennis courts at Moon Area High School, which was right behind my house—I'd dream up all sorts of fabulous finishes, perfect serves, and holes-in-one.

In basketball, I'd be a part of those great Boston Celtics teams of

95

the late 1960s and early 1970s. I'd be playing alongside John Havlicek and Bill Russell and putting up seventy points a game! I'd keep stats and set up crazy in-game scenarios. I never lost. Never! I loved it, and I remember how good it made me feel because all the thoughts I was having were positive ones.

There were many times when my mom would call me in for dinner, and I'd treat my next shot as if it were at the very end of the game. I'd count it down—FIVE, FOUR, THREE—I'd take a crazy fall away jumper always from the left corner over the backboard—TWO, ONE . . . If it went in, I'd run around screaming, hugging imaginary teammates and playing to the crowd. Then I'd head in to supper with a huge grin. My mom would be like, "What are you doing?"

If I missed the shot, an imaginary whistle would blow. "Foul, two shots." It was *my* dream, after all. I could make it as wacky as I wanted.

"Johnny, I'm not going to say it again . . . ," Mom would yell.

I would set up at the foul line. I made the first. Tie game. I'd dip, shoot . . . front rim, back rim, off the rim. TWEET. Lane violation! I'd sink the next free throw. It is my dream; I never let the game end on a down note. Why should I?

I always ate Mom's delicious meal with a good feeling, even if she was fuming about my being fifteen minutes late and letting the potatoes go cold.

The point of these little anecdotes isn't to show you how I kept myself amused in my younger years (although it sure was a lot better than the video games and instant messaging that's going on these days). No, the purpose of sharing these stories is for you to understand the need to have dreams and ambitions to drive you, especially throughout your bounce back. It's not just kids who dream big; it's adults like you too.

Whatever your dreams are, you need to be constantly envisioning them coming true in some way, shape, or form. I was never going to play in the NBA or on the pro tours in golf and tennis, but I had mental pictures of what success would be for me. Eventually, I got to the NBA—as a coach—and I've played golf and tennis with a few pros at various charity events!

Those dreams and others like them drove me, and I want you to have dreams of how you will turn the negative of your situation into a positive.

People often ask me, "How do you stay so positive *all* the time?" I tell them it's easy for me because I've always retained that vivid imagination that had me beating Ilie Năstase in tennis and Arnold Palmer in golf. As long as you are dreaming about where you want to be and what you want to accomplish, the positivity comes quite naturally.

The way my mom, Donna, put it was, "Dream big dreams, John. If you want to be the president of the United States, you can be."

> **PractiCal Point:** Dream big and don't let anyone tell you that your dreams are unrealistic; they are *your* dreams and you're entitled to each and every one.

· · ·

By now, you have surely picked up on my strong belief that a positive mental attitude is critically essential to making your bounce back story a "bestseller." In these initial months of settling into your bounce-back reentry opportunity, I want you to continually reach beyond your comfort zone. If you're fortunate enough to be in a spot where things are going smoothly, it's time to pursue greatness.

If things aren't going quite as efficiently, make the adjustments you need to make in order to continue on the right path.

I'm reminded of a preseason meeting I had with my UMass team prior to our Final Four campaign in 1995–96. We were coming off a 29–5 season, our fourth straight league title, and the school's first-ever Elite 8 appearance. The meeting was meant to establish some goals for us in the coming season. You've first got to understand we had lost three starters off the prior year's team (current UMass head coach Derek Kellogg, Lou Roe, and Mike Williams) *and* we were tackling what must have been the most ambitious schedule in the nation and one of the toughest ever.

Quite honestly, I was ready to temper expectations a bit when we started that meeting inside our locker room. In putting together the schedule, we knew we would take some lumps—especially early on—but we also knew every game would make us battle ready for the NCAA Tournament.

It was also a schedule made on the knowledge that preseason All-American junior Marcus Camby would be back as our starting center. With Marcus, we were going to win our fair share of games, and I figured we might as well play as many high-profile games as we could to showcase Marcus's skills and to prepare the team as a whole for pressure situations.

As I always do, I asked the team what they wanted our goals to be. Edgar Padilla, a junior guard, immediately yelled out, "Let's win the national title."

I loved it. *I have trained them well,* I thought. *Reach for the moon.* I began to write the goal on the dry-erase board and was interrupted by the bellowing voice of sophomore Tyrone Weeks.

"Let's go undefeated!" Ty said.

The statement stunned me and quieted the room a bit. A few of the players nodded in agreement, and a few voices said, "Yeah. Undefeated. That should be our goal."

"Whoa, whoa," I interrupted, hoping to settle things down a bit. "How about this? If we play our absolute hardest every game, play to the final horn, and play with our Refuse to Lose attitude, we can consider any losses as 'wins.'"

I felt it was necessary to have the team understand this was a daunting nonconference schedule—we had overscheduled for sure. I figured we'd be lucky to split our out-of-league games, and I would have been fine with that. As a coach, you have to accept the fact that you are going to lose games. We're just not going to win every game—it hasn't been done in college basketball since the 1976 Indiana team coached by Bobby Knight. Heck, years later, even the New England Patriots and Bill Belichick—a coach I truly admire— couldn't finish the deal in the 2007 season when they entered the Super Bowl at 18–0.

My rationale fell on deaf ears. The team was too excited about the prospect, and Tyrone—who wound up as an assistant with me at Memphis and is now at Marist with Chuck Martin—wouldn't let me off the hook.

"No, Coach, we want to win them *all*," he insisted.

It was a battle I didn't want to fight, and I remember rolling my eyes at my assistants when we broke for practice that afternoon. "Ty ruined a great meeting, didn't he?" I laughed. "Kid must be insane."

You know what, though? From his words, Ty instilled a vision quickly shared by everyone on the team. They were united in their dream to go undefeated, and I saw an energy in them that hadn't been there before.

Undefeated!?

Crazy kid.

Well, sure enough, we started off the year upsetting Kentucky by ten points in Detroit on November 28, 1995. By the end of December we were still undefeated and ranked No. 1 in the country. At the end of January, we had rattled off nineteen straight, and the national media started to latch onto the story and wonder if we could "pull an Indiana."

Maybe Tyrone Weeks wasn't so crazy after all.

But on February 24, 1996, with a 26–0 record, we hosted our league rival, George Washington, and the streak—and the pursuit of perfection—ended with an 86–76 loss.

Fact was, ever since Tyrone suggested going undefeated in our meeting, I had been thinking about what something like that could mean to our program and our university. It's still a dream of mine, to be quite honest. It's something no one thinks can be done, and I'd love to be the one that proves it can be accomplished.

The thing I had to do after the game was to let our guys know that 26–1 was still phenomenal. I told them our ultimate goal was to win the national championship, and that was still within our sights. The end result of that season was a Final Four berth for the first time in UMass history. In a national semifinal rematch with Kentucky, we made a spirited comeback and fell three points shy in the end.

It was a magical season, and it all started because one of our team members had the mettle to dream beyond anyone's wildest imagination. I'm glad they didn't let me off the hook at that initial meeting; sometimes the wildest ideas can yield the greatest results.

During our Final Four season at Memphis, a UMass graduate now living in Brookline, Massachusetts, sent me the African proverb Al Gore used upon accepting his Nobel Peace Prize in 2007, and it really hit home. "If you want to go quickly, go alone," Mr. Gore said. "If you want to go far, go together."

With your bounce back, we want to take it as far as possible, and we want to do it together.

> **PractiCal Point:** Realize there is nothing that is out of reach when you are part of a shared vision that serves as an inspiration to all involved.

• • •

Let me share another story with you. This one is about my younger cousin Matt from back when he was playing Little League baseball around the time he was about twelve years old.

Matt wasn't the most gifted player by any means, but he loved playing baseball and was always a hard worker and a great listener. His coaches always said they valued his enthusiasm and his "coach-ability." They played him in right field to protect him a bit.

Whenever I was back home, I tried to get to his games and see some of my other family and friends who attended all the town's sporting events. I would stand near the right-field fence to cheer Matt on and give him little pointers (once a coach, always a coach, I suppose).

Even at that young age, Matt had an attitude that never allowed him to get down, and he always believed in his team. I got a kick out of going to his games because he really had a great way of keeping things in perspective. Anyway, this one particularly scorching hot day I was about thirty minutes late to his game, and as I walked out to the fence, I asked Matt what inning they were in.

"First inning," he said.

"Did the game start late, Matt?"

"Nope. Right on time," he said, happily shooing flies.

"What's the score?" I asked, knowing things probably weren't going too well.

"Seventeen-nothing," he answered without a hint of frustration.

I was stunned. I couldn't think of anything to say to him. Turns out, I didn't have to.

"But," Matt gushed, "we haven't been up to bat yet!"

Here was a twelve-year-old kid, dripping sweat in the sweltering outfield in 90 percent humidity; his team was down seventeen runs, and there was still only one out in the top of the first, but Matt—God bless him—was just waiting for his team's turn at bat.

We've all been in situations similar to Matt's, but I'm guessing very few of us have been able to keep the power of positive thinking and blind faith Matt displayed in abundance. **I want you to dream like you're twelve years old again.** Have the attitude that there's nothing you cannot do. A twelve-year-old sees a fence keeping him from a ball field or a basketball court, and he says, "I'm going under it, I'm going over it, and if I have to, I'm lowering my shoulder and I'm going through it. There's nothing I can't do."

That's one of the most important themes I want you to take from this book: **Stay as positive and upbeat as you can possibly be. I'll say it many times: if you can dream it, you can be it.**

Like I said above, I want to coach a team before I retire that goes 40–0. One that wins *every* game. So you read that and think, *This dude needs drug testing. There's no way you can do that.*

Well, everybody tells me it can't be done, so that's my dream. I want to go 40–0; it's *my* dream, so it's perfectly rational.

PractiCal Point: Pursue your goals with the blissful determination and enthusiasm of a twelve-year-old.

. . .

The history books are filled with people who got knocked on their asses and had the fortitude to come back and not only survive their setbacks, but to thrive in life. I've been truly amazed by the names I've come across as I've researched this book. It's like a who's who of men and women who made this country great.

In my chosen field of coaching alone, the examples are endless. From Bill Belichick to Lou Holtz to Joe Torre, there's a long list of coaches who were once deemed too incompetent to lead and later went on to become dynasty builders and champions.

The more I read through these tales of comebacks by athletes, coaches, business leaders, and ordinary citizens, the more I discovered the common thread throughout: every person used the power of positivity to move forward. In spite of how crummy the situation seemed—be it Martha Stewart's public fall from grace or major-league baseball player Josh Hamilton's comeback from drug abuse—the affected person was able to take baby steps forward by remaining upbeat and resilient. They did not quit on themselves, and neither will you.

One of my former Memphis players, Darius Washington, who is from Orlando, Florida, is a testament to this notion. It was during my fifth season at Memphis in 2004–05, and we were coming off back-to-back NCAA Tournament appearances. The program was starting to get to a place where I knew we could compete for a national title every year, but we still had a ways to go, and I knew it. We had begun to crack the Top 25 polls with regularity the prior two seasons, but we had put ourselves in a bad position early and finished the regular season on a low, losing four conference games in a row against Charlotte, Louisville, Saint Louis, and Cincinnati.

So we went into the Conference USA Tournament, on our home floor at the FedExForum, with a 16–14 record and a No. 7 seed in the twelve-team field. We would need to win four games in three and a half days to make it back to the NCAA Tournament. We got things back together and won our first-round game against St. Louis and then took out No. 2 seed Charlotte in the quarterfinals. No. 11 seed South Florida had managed to advance to the semifinals, and we beat them, 81–68, to advance to my first C-USA championship game against our longtime rival and nemesis, No. 1 seed Louisville, which was ranked No. 9 in the nation.

The game was truly one of the hardest-fought games I had ever coached in. Big shot after big shot was the norm, and it appeared whoever had the ball last would win the game.

We trailed 75–73 with 6.7 seconds left. Darius dribbled the length of the court and launched a 3-pointer as time expired. The shot missed off the backboard, and the clock showed 0.0. But Darius got fouled on the shot by Louisville's Francisco Garcia and was awarded three free throws. Darius was a 72 percent free-throw shooter on the year, and he had made two of three during the game as part of his twenty-three-point performance. There was no one else on my team I would have wanted attempting those shots; he was our best free-throw shooter and tough as nails.

He calmly stepped to the line and swished the first shot to make it 75–74. Darius winked at the guys on the bench after he hit the first. His second shot hit the front rim, the back rim, and fell off. He could still tie the game and send it to overtime with his remaining free throw. I looked at Darius, gave him a little fist pump, and said, "Go ahead," as he stepped to the line.

The CBS color analyst doing the game, Jim Spanarkel, said to the national TV audience, "You can't describe the pressure here."

And you couldn't. It was dead quiet, and since we were playing in our home gym, most of the crowd were praying for Darius.

Darius dipped, he shot, and the ball bounced twice on the front of the rim and fell to the floor. As the Louisville team celebrated its automatic berth to the NCAA Tournament, Darius fell at the foul line, brought his jersey over his face, and collapsed on his stomach. He was inconsolable.

It all played out right in front of our bench, so I was able to immediately get out and, with the help of a player and a coach, get Darius to his feet. He was despondent, and the image of him lying on the floor in anguish for several seconds was one that was played over and over again on the highlight shows.

He could barely walk off the floor. At nineteen years old, Darius Washington had just experienced a crushing defeat in front of thousands of fans in the arena and hundreds of thousands more watching on television. It would be hours, literally, before the kid would stop sobbing in the locker room. I had never seen a player so shaken.

The night of the Louisville loss, Darius took a walk down Beale Street with his dad, Darius Sr. "That was a risky move," Darius Sr. said in an October 17, 2005, *Sports Illustrated* (*SI*) article written by the talented Grant Wahl, "but when [we] did [it], everybody just mobbed him. 'Don't worry about it! We'll get 'em next time!' Nothing negative. We were just letting [the fans] know that [Darius was] not going to run and hide from this." Darius's misses meant we would miss out on the NCAA Tournament. But our program at Memphis owed a lot of its identity to the way Darius handled that situation. Instead of becoming a source of ridicule or scorn, Darius became a rallying point for not just our city but for hundreds, if not thousands, of people across the country. His bounce-back story was inspirational. In that *SI* article, Wahl wrote:

> More than 100 letters poured into the Tigers' basketball office: notes from Tennessee congressman Harold Ford and Temple coach John Chaney, a get-well card from Louisville fans, a letter signed by 32 members of a men's prayer group, a sticker collage from a four-year-old girl, a handwritten 3,000-word missive from a prison inmate on the meaning of failure and enough citations of Romans 8:28 and Jeremiah 29:11–14 to start a revival meeting.
>
> Meanwhile, the messages were piling up on DWash.net, Washington's website:
>
> From hbengal: "Your heart & desire are what sports are all about. I was moved to tears, not for the loss but because I cared about you!"
>
> From Tigerlover: "My boys have a new hero. . . . I picked them up at school today, and my six-year-old wanted to hurry home so he could play his video game: 'I am going to be Darius and I am going to win the national championship so he won't be sad anymore.'"

The one thing I did with Darius the day after the game was to make him join me on a national TV interview to discuss the missed shots. He didn't want to do it. He wanted to stay under the covers, but after some cajoling and persuading, he agreed.

Now, you might be thinking that was cruel to do to the kid. But that was not my intention, and Darius knew it. I needed him to see that life goes on, that the sun will rise and the sun will set and life would move on.

"Everyone knows of you," I remember telling him, "and everyone feels for you. By doing this interview and showing how strong you are, you will prove to people how resilient you are. You will show them that if there's ever a situation like that again, you are not only going to embrace it, but you are going to make the shots."

"If I didn't have positive people around me, I would have gone into a shell," Darius Jr. said in the *SI* article. "My dad said, 'You have to go outside [eventually], so you might as well do it now so everyone can see you.' One day a little kid came up to me and said, 'Ain't you the dude who missed those free throws? How could you miss those?' I just said, 'Keep living. Things don't always come out how you want them.'"

For me the entire sequence of events after Darius's misses was a learning process. What an incredible lesson that whole situation became for me and our program.

You just never know what your setback is going to ignite as far as future results go.

The next season, we went 33–4 and made it to the Elite 8 of the NCAAs with Darius at the point. He was our team's second-leading scorer and made the most free throws for us that year. He wound up putting his name in the NBA draft following that season and has gone on to a successful career overseas, and he has also had a few cups of coffee in the NBA.

When I think of the power of being positive and the way it can propel you to greatness, I think not of Darius's missed free throw, but of the constructive way he handled its fallout. I don't think it's out of bounds to say that Darius got more out of that "failure" than he ever would have gotten from helping us to the NCAA Tournament.

> **PractiCal Point:** Appreciate the unexpected outcomes your trigger event will lead to and whom you will affect.

• • •

Now is the time for you to reach out—with clarity and passion—to both the "Yes, you can" encouragers in your life and the firm, tough-love Kitchen Cabinet you identified in Practice Plan #1.

In order to get the absolute maximum out of your support-system members, you first need to have a skeletal outline of how you want these people to help you. It is disrespectful to use the time of cherished confidants you are contacting and not have specific questions and requests in mind when you speak or meet with them.

You have to show that you are willing to help yourself before others are going to take an active role in helping you; more important, you have to *be* willing to help yourself before others are going to take an active role in helping you. I can't stress the importance of this enough.

"If you reach out to people too quickly after a [job] loss and you are still angry and upset and you share that with people, those people are going to say, 'Whoa. This guy's got a lot of baggage,'" said career coach Bobbie LaPorte. "You've got to get through that point and take a different attitude and start to turn things around especially when you are dealing with those who can be valuable contacts for you in your [bounce back]."

There are hundreds of people just waiting to help you, but they need to be engaged and made to feel a part of the process.

Let me tell you what I did before reaching out to my Kitchen

Cabinet after the Nets firing, and hopefully you can glean some tips and ideas from my approach.

Because of the timing of my firing (in the middle of the NBA season, toward the end of the college basketball season), I knew I wouldn't be able to get another job coaching right away. I also knew I needed some time to recharge my batteries and create a solid game plan for how I would reenter the coaching world.

Here were some of my primary concerns:

- About a week after the Nets let me go, I had the good fortune of being approached by ESPN to work on a weekly NBA show called *NBA Matchup*. I jumped at the opportunity, and after getting comfortable with my role, I started to think that maybe I could do TV work for a few years. I wondered if my Kitchen Cabinet would think it was a good idea for me to get into broadcasting full-time.
- I wondered if it might be good to just take an entire year away from the game altogether. But I wasn't sold on that, so I put it down on my list of things to discuss with my Kitchen Cabinet.
- Even with television as an option, I was pretty sure I wanted to get back into coaching full-time, but I wasn't as sure about what path to take. I thought long and hard about whether it was in my best interest—and my family's—to go back to the college game or try and stick with the NBA in some capacity. That, too, was an important question for my Cabinet to help answer.

It would be crucial for me to hear what my Kitchen Cabinet thought about the pro vs. college question. I had a feeling I knew what they were going to say, but I didn't let that preclude me from asking. I think that's important; sometimes we're so convinced we know how a person is thinking that we completely neglect to ask—and listen to—their way of thinking.

If you don't ask, you won't know for sure.

To be honest, I was 90 percent sure that going back to the *right* college situation was going to be my best option. As you'll see from my experience, however, there's no predicting how things will turn out.

There were other concerns as well, and I made sure to include them on my list of topics for the Cabinet members:

- What should I be doing to help my former assistants and staff who were also terminated by the Nets organization?
- Had my image been tarnished so dramatically that I would need some kind of "revival campaign" in order to restore my status? If not, who would defend me? (As I would soon find out, Coach Brown would be my staunchest defender.)
- Lastly, I had to seriously consider whether it was time to get out of coaching for good. This wasn't something I was truly considering, but it was something I wanted to toss around with my Kitchen Cabinet, just to gauge their thoughts.

Once I had all those questions written down and organized, I was ready to begin contacting my Kitchen Cabinet.

PractiCal Point: Write down what you are going to discuss with your Kitchen Cabinet (or others) and prioritize that list.

• • •

A word of caution, though, before you start making your plans with your Kitchen Cabinet: remember that these are important people in your life, so make sure they know that you care about them as much as you're asking them to care about you. Show a genuine interest in how they are and what they are up to. I've said this before, and it bears repeating: you're not the only one going through some sort of life obstacle. While yours may seem bigger and worse than anyone else's, chances are it is quite comparable to what friends, associates, and relatives are dealing with in their own lives.

So, every conversation I had, I would start off by asking, "How are you doing today? Is everything going okay with you?"

Let's face it; most of your closest sounding boards aren't going to allow you to feel pity for them—especially when they know you're going through a tough stretch. But the simple fact is, you are showing interest in them and letting them know you're not selfish. Support is a two-way street, and it's essential that your Kitchen Cabinet members understand that, however low you may be, you still have enough compassion and sense to care about their circumstances.

Now, it's quite likely you have already been communicating with your Cabinet since the trigger event took place—I encourage that fully. Depending on your relationship with each member, they are probably keenly aware of what you have been going through and how you have been dealing with the initial phases. Your job now is to be sure you explain, in no uncertain terms, that you are going to be leaning heavily on them for guidance and "coaching." You want to be sure they know that they are going to be integral members of your bounce-back team and that you are expecting them to be as brutally honest as they can possibly be. If you sense any apprehension on any Cabinet member's part to play this role for you, you need to recognize it and replace him or her as a Cabinet member.

One thing that really struck me as I started to get back into circulation and reconnect with those I thought were my friends and supporters was how fleeting fake friendships can be. When I began to make calls to discover some of my options after the Nets, I immediately discovered the difference between an acquaintance and a true friend. There is no better time to find out where people stand with you than when you're getting up off the mat. I learned not to be disappointed or upset when some people didn't return my calls, even people I had helped in the past. Some relationships we have are relationships of convenience. (That being the case, I have tried to move on when I realized that I was befriended by someone because of my position.)

At the end of the day, we have to be responsible for ourselves. **You must be an active participant in your survival.**

But the involvement and interest from your Kitchen Cabinet allows you to realize they are with you every step of the way. Take pride in knowing people care about you that deeply.

> **PractiCal Point:** Let your Kitchen Cabinet know you value their opinions and can't have them being afraid to speak their minds.

• • •

As long as you are comfortable with the list of topics you have put together for the members of your Cabinet, it's now time to begin reaching out to them. Again, let me emphasize you need to be completely ready before you start placing phone calls and taking meetings.

It's also important to be clear about what you want from your KC and what they can expect from you as you proceed. That way, career coach Bobbie LaPorte said, "People are able to respond and go, 'Okay, I see what you want, and you have really taken the time to think about your next step.' There, they see you have been thoughtful and you are respecting their time."

This is all about communicating—not just verbally communicating either. It's through body language, your actions, and the way you treat and respond to people. Throughout my career I have come to realize and understand the value of open and honest communication. Through it, trust is built and enhanced. Part of the trust that develops from communication is becoming comfortable with knowing that even though you are swinging for fences, there will be times when you will strike out.

I find communicating to our players about how they benefit from playing on a team with national-title ambitions is very important. I do it early on every season to make sure we are all pulling in the same direction. I explain thoroughly how each of us benefits as the team rises. Playing on the last day of the season creates opportunities for four or five members of each team because of the exposure and recognition it creates for the young men.

I put the ability to motivate others at the very top of the list of a coach's greatest assets. When I say that, I'm talking about not just the capacity to stimulate players to be the best they can be, but also the knack for motivating staff, administrators, and the community at large. And in this phase, you need to be able to invigorate the people around you, especially your Kitchen Cabinet, so that they can do the same for you.

You want to have a collection of people who are not only working on your behalf and providing sound advice, but who can take pride in your bounce back, the way our school and our city takes pride in our program. You have to help them help you.

In order for your KC to feel that gratification of watching you bounce back, you need to keep that upbeat, positive attitude that we have been discussing throughout this book. My old boss at UMass and great friend, Bob Marcum, told me he remembered back to the first days and weeks after the Nets let me go. Bob said I would call him often—usually at some odd hour—but despite what had been going on, he marveled at the way I stayed upbeat. "You just don't have too many highs and lows, John," he said to me at one point. "You're always optimistic and even-keeled."

That meant a lot to me coming from Bob, who has been one of college athletics' most respected and most levelheaded leaders throughout his career. He retired as Marshall University's AD in the summer of 2009, and I'm happy to say that will afford him the opportunity to spend some time with me in Lexington.

My true friends were—and still are—a small group whom I could count on for an honest appraisal and constructive criticism. Don't get pouty and show indignation when you are told something you don't want to hear. It's on you to accept the advice and use it to better yourself and your situation.

You want to elicit feedback like that from your own Kitchen Cabinet, and the best way to do that is to ooze the positivity and confidence that will automatically engage them and make them proud to be members of your team.

PractiCal Point: Purposely allowing frank and direct communications with those around you benefits not only your bounce back but the overall morale and input of everyone you are leaning on.

WRITE YOUR OWN STORY

Before we delve deeper into the second distinct phase of your bounce-back where you will carefully plot your course and ultimately establish your bounce-back opportunity, it's time for you to undertake what I see as the single most important coaching session of your bounce back.

Notice I have not labeled this a Practice Plan, and instead I'm presenting it as an individual meeting—just me and you—in my office, door closed, nothing off-limits.

From time to time during a season or in the off-season, I will sit down in this manner, one-on-one, with each of my players (and my staff) and really get into each one's psyche and try and determine where each person is in his development. For the younger players, we're looking at how they're adapting to college life, our system, and the demands and expectations of being in our program. For the upperclassmen, we're assessing how they've progressed from season to season, what kind of leaders they are becoming, and what they're hoping to get out of their final year or two.

I suppose the business world equivalent of this would be an annual performance review, but my one-on-ones are a bit different. The discussions are not solely performance based; instead we're looking at reviewing where each player or coach is in the course of fulfilling his dreams and aspirations.

As much as I'd love to sit down face-to-face with each and every reader of this book—hundreds of thousands of you, we hope!—and discuss what your plans are for your "second life" (a concept you will learn more about in chapter 11), I am instead going to ask you to do something I had great success with during our Final Four season of 2007–08. It's called "Writing Your Own Story," and it picked up a lot of national attention because of my senior center, Joey Dorsey.

As with each coaching session and practice plan in this book, after you write your story, I welcome you to share it—or portions of it—at **www.coachcalbounceback.com.** I envision thousands and thousands of stories at the website from which everyone in our bounce-back community can gain stimulation, inspiration, and motivation.

Let me first explain a bit about Joey Dorsey to you and then the concept itself, after which I will send you off on your own to create your own beautiful and bountiful bounce-back story:

• • •

It's still up for debate whether Joey Dorsey is the player I spent the most time yelling at over a four-year career. You can safely assume he's in the top three. He's also tops among my all-time-favorite players I've coached—and that's not a list I'm even comfortable talking about because I've loved all my players for different reasons and in different ways.

Did Joey try my patience at times? You could say that. Did he make some awfully silly and immature decisions during his time in Memphis? No question. Did he finally put it all together when it counted most? Yes, he did, and in the process he became an adopted Memphian who will always be loved in that city.

I love Joey too, like a son. But while he was at Memphis, he did some of the dumbest things I've ever seen in my whole life. I'm not going to get into his transgressions, but let's just say like my man Frank Sinatra sang, "Regrets, [he] had a few!" Joey has matured through all of it, and when he left campus, he was a wiser man and not the sometimes foolish kid he came in as. He learned from those public mistakes, and he grew from them—that's all you can ask of anyone.

Joey had grown up in a Baltimore neighborhood like the ones depicted so vividly in the fabulous HBO series *The Wire*. There were security cameras on every street corner's telephone pole, drugs flowing in the streets, crime, gangs, and the bleakest of environments in which to grow up. Joey was the first member of his family to graduate from high school and the first to finish college as well. When we got him at Memphis, he was raw and a bit rough around the edges.

"My freshman year [2004–05], Coach Cal would be yelling at me, and I wasn't even playing!" Joey said. "It took a while for me to understand he was teaching me—trying to make me better. My team-mates had to keep explaining to me he was showing he cared."

In fact, Ellen would always complain to me, "Quit yelling at Joey so much. Spread it around, would you?"

Thing is, Joey was very much like my own child. I think of it this way: I can yell at Bradley, Erin, or Megan, and I can call out their faults or missteps because they're *my* kids. But if someone else tries that? Uh-uh. Not gonna fly. It was the same way with Joey—it was okay for me to get all over him and scream like a maniac at him during games or practice, but if anyone else started picking him apart or questioning him, I'd be Joey's biggest defender.

For the longest time, Joey didn't think he deserved to be where he was. He was expecting bad things to happen to him. He could only think his future would eventually bring him back to the streets of Baltimore where he would wind up a statistic, a has-been, or a failure. We had to get him to believe that he deserved not only good things but great things. I give a lot of credit to my assistant John Robic in that regard. He took a special interest in Joey, and they developed a bond where Joey could go to Robes on anything—basketball or life issues. I know Robes takes pride in the relationship he built with Joey, and that, too, is a great lesson for you. **Sometimes, the greatest thing you can do for yourself is to help someone else achieve greatness.**

I once watched a TV show on Johnny Cash, and one of the things Johnny did was he wrote his own story every year. It served as a sort of prediction and vision for what he would accomplish in the coming year.

I'd heard of people who wrote their own obituaries in the middle of their lives and tried to live up to them, or others who had written their epitaphs, but that always struck me as a bit bleak, too morbid for my liking. The idea of writing your own story and living to fulfill *that* story resonated much more with me. It was a positive way of funneling your dreams and desires into a series of paragraphs that you could always refer back to whenever you needed a boost or perspective. I stored the idea away and knew there would be an opportunity at some point to use it with my team.

When Joey started to slump in his senior year (2007–08), it seemed to be the perfect opening to test out the concept.

In my individual meeting with him, I handed him a brand-new blue spiral notebook with the Memphis logo embossed on the cover.

"What's this for, Coach?" Joey asked.

"Joey, this is it—your final run," I said. "I want you to take this notebook and write your own story. I want you to write how you want your regular season to end. It's your fairy tale, it's your dream, write it. Maybe the team carries you off the court because you made the game-winning free throws. (That was an inside joke because Joey was a career 42 percent free-throw shooter for us.) Maybe the crowd chants your name as you leave the arena. Whatever it is—however wacky or far-out it may be—just write it in this notebook. It needs to touch on everything, paragraph by paragraph."

I could see Joey begin to fantasize about what his ultimate scenario would be. I knew I had connected with him, and I paused a second to give silent thanks to the Man in Black—we were walking the line together. I then asked Joey, once he had written his own story, to read it over and over and over, my purpose being if he read it enough and believed in it enough, he could make it happen.

In our final two regular-season games, Joey scored twenty-two points and grabbed twenty rebounds in forty-six total minutes. On senior night against UAB, the fans did, indeed, chant his name. "JO-EY! JO-EY! JO-EY!" they screamed, and you could see how it touched him. It worked so well, in fact, that come NCAA Tournament time, I had Joey write his own story again. Just before the tournament, Joey told me he had written his new ending. I never asked him to share it with me, and when the media got hold of the story, Joey wouldn't share what he had written. "I'm not telling," he said. "I'll tell y'all after it comes true." (Although he did allow some of us a brief peek into his writings he completed before the national semifinal game against UCLA. He had handwritten a one-page story he called, "No Love for UCLA." It described how he would redeem himself and his team for the smack he had unwisely spoken on Greg Oden the year before. It was some pretty inspirational writing as he dominated the glass that night with a game-high fifteen rebounds in twenty-seven minutes while helping to hold UCLA big man Kevin Love to twelve points and nine rebounds.)

All through the season and especially in the postseason, I was telling the entire team, "I want you to expect good things to happen because your only other option is to wait for bad things to happen."

The same holds true for you in your bounce back: **You deserve good things and you need to expect them—every day and in every situation.**

Joey's story for the end of his incredible career as a Tiger couldn't have been written any better. He was drafted No. 33 overall in the 2008 NBA draft, winding up with Houston. He lived up to his story and realized his dreams.

Now it's your turn to make like Joey.

I want you to get your own blue spiral notebook, and I want you to go paragraph by paragraph, clearly spelling out the path you see your life taking as your bounce back unfolds. The more comprehensive and the more specific you make it, the more beneficial it will be in the long run. This story you are composing shouldn't be plotted out too far in the future. Set up a reasonable time frame for your story to take place in—maybe a year or eighteen months. If you plot too far ahead, you risk writing a fairy tale.

The beauty of writing your own story is that you can rewrite it, write a whole new one, or edit what you have at any time during your bounce back and the remainder of your inspiring life.

Don't fear if you're not a writer—you don't have to be. The passion from your heart and the inspiration from your mind will make your story a bestseller whatever the grammar, punctuation, or style is. I'm serious about that—I've worked at my writing over the years, and my ability to get my thoughts and ideas down on paper has been an invaluable asset as I've moved up through the coaching ranks. I couldn't have done this book without continuously working on and improving my writing style through repetition and practice.

Remember this: even if some people love to see the mighty fall, everyone loves a comeback story. What are the most popular movies every year? I'm thinking of *Seabiscuit, Hoosiers, Cinderella Man, Pursuit of Happyness* (I cried like a baby at that one).

Write your own tear-jerker, your own uplifting tale of determination. Once you've got it written, read it over a few times so you begin to live to that story—your goal is to make the words on the paper come to life.

Then, I want you to go to **www.coachcalbounceback.com** and share as much of your story as you are comfortable with so we can all experience the joy of watching dreams come true.

Here are six themes that may be helpful for you to include as you partake in this monumentally important exercise.

What will make you happiest?

Think about times in your life when you were most happy, and consider the circumstances around those times. Let your story include a paragraph on what happiness means to you and how you are going to achieve it.

How will you take charge of your life?

I think it's important to have a paragraph or two about the manner in which you're going to live your new life and the guidelines you will follow. This can include your diet, eliminating vices, and maybe your exercise program—things that prove to yourself you are in control. This is also where you can delve into the acceptance of what has taken you to this point and your strength to put everything behind you with *no regrets*.

Why are you putting yourself on this path?

What is your motivation? More important, have you learned from your past transgressions or missteps? Do not let your story be a rewrite of an old tale. This has to be a fresh, new perspective on the new you you're creating. Look within, and ask yourself what new experiences you will take on and how dedicated you will become to those adventures.

When will you know that you're headed in the right direction?

What will be signals to your mind and your heart that you have made strides? Will it be the relationships you have, the money you earn, or the power of your resiliency? Think about those things carefully, and don't underestimate the value of loving yourself. Also, remember you cannot waste time as you move forward. Don't allow for any stagnation in your bounce back. Idle time is wasted time. If it helps, devise a timeline and highlight target dates for when you will accomplish distinct goals within your bounce back.

Whom will you share your successes and joys with?

One of the most fulfilling parts of your bounce back will be when you reach milestones and are able to share those achievements with others. Include a paragraph about what you will do to uplift others through your accomplishments. Make sure you include the same people who were there for you in the toughest of times—they will take as much pride in your bounce back as you will.

How will you impact others?

This should be the closing paragraph to your own amazing story. What will you do to help others around you or even complete strangers? Only when you are able and willing to help others can your bounce back be fulfilled.

SECTION II

. . .

GO
FOR
IT

CHAPTER 7

BUILD YOUR SELF-WORTH

HELP OTHERS TO HELP YOURSELF

You have come through the nonconference schedule of your bounce back in great shape. This next portion of your journey will coincide with what my teams experience during the conference play of any given season.

Think about this for a minute: when you first became a member of my bounce-back team, you were a little bit lost. You were searching for answers and wondering—likely for the first time—how you were going to deal with the emotional and trying event you were experiencing. Through the six chapters—your own "nonconference" schedule of games—you have been able to wrestle control of your situation and take the steps necessary to make your bounce-back story the greatest it can be.

I bet there were times in the first couple of chapters when you had little faith and couldn't see any good in anything. There may have been instances where you put the book down altogether and said, "To hell with it, Coach!"

Those are perfectly natural segments of your bounce back. The urge to quit instead of charging forward is more than understandable. But you fought that urge. Look at yourself. You haven't quit, and you will not quit! Each day that passes from your trigger event is another day you have been able to move forward—however small you may think your steps have been.

I know it hasn't been easy, and I know I have been asking a lot out of you. I have been throwing things at you that might not make sense now but will later. You have to be able to look back—in a few days or a few weeks—and realize that you are on the road to recovery and that together we are doing everything in our collective power to correct your situation. You are stronger than you ever imagined, and you will continue to gain strength each day you are on my team.

So please know that I am full of pride over what you have been able to accomplish so far, and I am genuinely excited by what the future has in store for us as we enter the "conference schedule."

• • •

League play in college basketball mostly starts in early January after the bulk of nonconference matchups are completed. (I'm actually one of the few coaches in the country who likes to schedule a late-season nonconference game. I do it as another way to prepare my team for the NCAA Tournament.)

The conference games are crucial for many reasons. The better you do in-league, the better your seed will be in the conference tournament, where the champion receives an automatic bid to the NCAA Tournament. The conference games are also vital for creating momentum for the end of the season when you hope to be playing your best basketball. Lastly—and this holds true especially for a team like mine that has had so much national success—the conference games are often played against bitter rivals, and road games become miniwars where it's the guys on our bench against the opponent's hostile, frothing crowd intent on seeing us lose.

For your bounce back, these next few weeks and months of "conference play" will determine how much success you have in your own personal postseason. Because of that, I'm going to be asking a lot of you in the coming chapters. You may feel overwhelmed by the amount of effort I will be expecting from you. Again, I want you to remember your bounce back will move at your own pace, but if you are truly serious about getting yourself out of the rut or turmoil you now find yourself in, you're going to need to step it up and, of course, keep that positive outlook I have been emphasizing throughout.

Let's get into a little bit of what it is I expect from my team during the conference schedule and how that will coincide with what I am expecting from you during this stretch of your bounce back.

By the time the conference portion of our season rolls around, we have been together for three months, and all my players and staff members are in good positions to sit down and objectively look at where they have come in ninety days and where they hope to go in the next ninety days.

I see this as being very similar to where you are in your bounce back. You have had time to get over the initial shock, you have had time to reflect and assess, and, most important, you have been able to cultivate a relentlessly positive outlook.

But let's first be sure that you're strong enough and adequately prepared to delve into the difficult task of finding your reentry opportunity. I can almost see you shaking your head and questioning how I expect you to know if you're mentally prepared for the weeks and months ahead—days that are bound to be filled with leaps forward and bounds backward.

The best way to confirm this is by growing your self-confidence and reinforcing it in several manners. Start doing this now and continue it throughout your entire bounce back.

There are a few things you can do to prove to yourself that you can bounce back—and at the same time steel yourself for the upcoming battles you will face in furthering your bounce back.

First, remember this: **Being down is only permanent if you make it that way.** You control your destiny in every way, shape, and form. If you're not strong enough to understand that at this moment, place your faith in me, because I *know* you have the fortitude. We all do—sometimes we just have to discover it from within.

This is when you need to have blind faith in your abilities. Whatever you've done up to this point in your life is significant. Whether you were a CEO, a salesperson, or a manager, you worked to get where you were and showed resiliency and initiative in achieving your rank. If you were in a relationship, that partnership took time and effort to build, and you obviously were part of the reason it developed into something special.

What I'm saying is there's no reason you can't again reach whatever level you were at when you were satisfied and content with your career or your personal life. If you were a senior-level professional before, then by all means you can reach that same position with a different company. If you had happiness and joy and love, there's no reason you can't experience those emotions again. If you've been there once, you will get there again. **You have to expect good things to happen in order for them to actually occur.**

I had to realize that after the Nets fired me, and it did take some time, but the more I looked at everything around me, the more I realized I was still the same person who had resurrected the UMass program, established legitimacy in New Jersey, and built a successful career brick by brick. I began to realize the firing was going to make me more complete and, in the long run, a much better person and a much wiser coach.

The only way you can come out swinging for your next opportunity is to feel really good about yourself. Sometimes you have to be pushed into a corner in order to see just how strong you are. When that happens, and you feel like you're in the void, you can either be all done and stay in the abyss or you can be positive and confident and climb out.

There is absolutely nothing to be gained from feeling sorry for yourself, and I do not allow my players the opportunity to do that. I hold them accountable, and I want you to be accountable as well. Do not cheat yourself by cutting corners or taking the easy way out—it will come back to bite you in the end, I guarantee it.

> **PractiCal Point:** Realize you've been to the mountaintop before, and you can get there again.

• • •

Another effective mechanism for guaranteeing you're capable of entering this next phase is to find significance again through any means possible. I was able to do this after the Nets—and after the Kansas loss—by doing things for others. In fact, it was when I began to devote my time and effort to making the lives of people around me better that I truly began to feel as though my bounce back was on the right path. Whether it was helping my assistants reach their goals or making sure my secretary would be able to provide a quality education for her son or daughter, I became a better person and a better leader when I knew I was helping others and saw the way it affected them.

I want you to do something for others.

So often when we are dealt a major blow in our professional or personal lives, we tend to become isolated and removed from the regular day-to-day things we have been attached to. There's a stigma associated with job loss or personal strife, and because of that, human nature often dictates that we become more isolated.

I know that with job loss—and I think separation and divorce as well—there's a tendency to lose your identity. That self-worth you had, which was in many ways tied into your career or your significant other, is all of a sudden gone. It can be an odd, bewildering sensation, to say the least.

The experts tell us this is probably more common in men and quite prevalent with high-ranking leaders of industry because their identities are tightly woven into their jobs or job titles. But as more and more women become leaders of industry, the same phenomenon affects them.

The fact you are going through a rough patch should not, in any way, keep you from being a productive, contributing member of society. In fact, this is a golden opportunity for you to get involved with some organizations or projects that you may not have had time for in the past.

I'm not just talking about getting physically fit or lowering your golf handicap either. I'm talking about taking on tasks that both make *you* feel significant again and will also make a significant impact on *others*.

Some of it can be charitable work, and some of it might be getting more involved with your church or temple. Isn't it peculiar how we gravitate toward our faith when we are down and then tend to pull back when things are going smoothly? I encourage you to use this time in your life as an opportunity to find consistency within your religious practices.

Another useful way to find significance again is through volunteering. Not only will you feel good about yourself after helping out at a local homeless shelter or in a hospital, but I guarantee that experiences like that will give you some valuable perspective on the circumstances of your own situation. Ellen has taught me the value of volunteering through her work with local schoolchildren.

Being part of the community is such an integral part of rediscovering the world around you when you're getting into your bounce back. It will give you perspective and help you feel like a contributing member of society again. As we get older and wiser, we should all come to the conclusion that our own legacies will be more about whom we have touched and helped than they will be about our own accomplishments. With each passing year it becomes a more important focus for me.

Not only will your spirit be lifted to a place where you understand what a special person you are, your good deeds will also become something you yearn to do even after you have achieved your reentry opportunity.

Mahatma Gandhi's pledge of "My life is my message" sums it up best of all. Even as we go through our own tough times, our emotional well-being is, in many ways, tied to others. As you help others, you help yourself in immeasurable and impactful ways.

During our Final Four season at Memphis, one of my guards, a sophomore and a Bluff City native, Willie Kemp, hosted his kindergarten teacher at one of our home games. He had never forgotten the woman, and she had been ailing lately, so when Willie heard that, he took matters into his own hands and treated her like a queen for that night. Not only did Willie get her tickets and talk to her before the game, but my secretary, Lunetha Pryor, heard about what Willie had done, and she arranged to have the teacher sit right behind the bench.

The story spread when a columnist in town wrote about it.

It was one of those "pay it forward"–type moments, and it showed what surrounding yourself with good people—at all levels—can really do for you and your organization. After that game, I told all the players they needed to go and thank someone the same way Willie had.

"Call one or more persons in your life who have made a difference for you," I said. "Call them and thank them. Maybe it's your parents who gave up everything to get you to college or someone who believed in you when no one else believed in you. Call that person or persons and thank them."

Four of my guys came back a few days later and said they had made the person they called cry. How about that?

You will be amazed at what it will do for you during your own bounce back to know you are making a difference in the lives of others.

Whenever I think of how crucial it is to give back, I think of people like my good friends Mark B. Fisher and Paul Tudor Jones II and their incredible charitable and community-based endeavors.

I've known Mark since our UMass days. He's been a longtime, successful commodities broker and is the founder and CEO of MBF Clearing Corp., a huge player in the global futures market. (He's also an author of the fascinating book *The Logical Trader: Applying a Method to the Madness*.) In the 1980s, after graduating from the Wharton School, Mark became the youngest person—at twenty-one years old—ever to trade in the silver futures pit.

With all his successes and influential practices, Mark's greatest achievements may be his philanthropic endeavors. Every summer, a select group of young men and women, including apprentice traders, accomplished students, and scholar-athletes, as well as disadvantaged youth from throughout the New York metropolitan area, attend Mark's internship program. In fact, I had three former UMass players go through the program (Carmelo Travieso, Dana Dingle, and Charlton Clarke).

Paul is another incredibly giving and kind soul. I met him through Mark, and wouldn't you know it, he's a native Memphian and someone I leaned on heavily when I was making my decision on whether or not to take the Memphis job. In 2008, *Forbes* listed Paul in the Top 350 of the world's billionaires and estimated his worth at $3.3 billion. He's the president and founder of Tudor Investment Corporation and is widely recognized as one of the world's best-known and richest hedge-fund managers.

As with Mark, it's Paul's philanthropic interests that truly set him apart. In 1987, Paul founded the Robin Hood Foundation, a nonprofit dedicated to aiding New York City's impoverished citizens. I remember going to one of the foundation's annual dinners, and I was completely blown away by the fund-raising and spirit lifting that Paul has spearheaded. In fact, in one single banquet a couple of years ago, Paul's foundation raised $70 million. In one night!

When I look at both Mark and Paul and others like them, it always brings a question to my mind: how do some of the most successful business minds in the world find the time to do things that the rest of us claim we don't have time for?

The answer I come to is that these leaders of industry yearn to find significance beyond what they already have accomplished.

That's a valuable lesson for you to take forward during—and after—your bounce back.

> **PractiCal Point:** Find significance again through charitable endeavors or some type of community involvement, and make giving to others a priority in your life.

· · ·

I discovered the power of helping others early in my career, and thankfully it has stayed with me ever since. In the 1984–85 season while I was at Kansas under Coach Brown, we had landed a prized recruit out of Omaha named Cedric Hunter. Cedric was a six-foot, 180-pound guard who was just an absolutely stupefying athlete. There was nothing he couldn't do on the basketball court—he jumped center in high school but played guard, and in his senior year he averaged twenty-seven points per game.

When Cedric got to campus, Coach Brown decided he wanted him to be our point guard, and I was entrusted with the job of working with Cedric. Every day before practice we would work on all sorts of drills and moves he could add to his already impressive skill set. He was such a great kid and a competitor like almost no one I'd ever seen. He owned the court every time he played, and we wanted to make sure he had plenty of moves in his arsenal.

In our individual work sessions, I was careful not to add things that might lead to unnecessary turnovers in the rough and tumble Big 8.

My greatest thrill—it gives me goose bumps just thinking about it—was during one league game when Cedric perfectly executed a play we had been working on all that week in our sessions. When he turned to run back down court on defense, he looked over to the bench and pointed to me as if I were the one who made the move. I almost felt like I did!

It remains one of the most fulfilling experiences in my entire coaching career. Is there anything better than someone's accomplishing things that were previously out of his reach and then acknowledging your impact when he conquers the task?

I had a similar thrill during the first round of the 2009 NBA Playoffs. My former point guard at Memphis, Derrick Rose, had been named the league's Rookie of the Year, and his team, the Chicago Bulls, was going to present him his trophy before a playoff game against Boston.

A day before the game, I got a call from Derrick.

"Coach," he said in his quiet way, "what are you doing tomorrow night?"

I had a few things going on in Lexington but nothing that I couldn't reschedule.

"Nothing much," I told him.

"I was hoping you could come to our game," he said. "They're giving me the Rookie award."

I didn't hesitate. "Of course I'll be there," I said.

We talked for a while more, and I told him how proud I was of him. I got off the phone, and I was honestly near tears. In the course of two years, Derrick had gone from a shy, skinny freshman to a leader on our Final Four team, then to the No. 1 overall pick in the 2008 NBA draft, and now to the best rookie in the league. He has accomplished so much and still has many years ahead of him to form into who I think will be one of the all-time great point guards. To know I played a small part in helping him reach some of his dreams means the world to me. Then to have him take the time to call and make sure I'd be there with him on his special night?

That's what this is all about, folks. Ten years earlier, I didn't know if I'd ever coach again, but in April 2009, I was sitting in the United Center watching one of my "prized pupils" as the head coach of the Kentucky Wildcats.

All I could say was, "Wow."

It made me think back to what the late psychiatrist, author, and radio host David Viscott once said: **"The purpose of life is to discover your gift. The meaning of life is to give your gift away."**

I know that ability and drive are within you, and I know that you have developed and blossomed through the course of your bounce back.

• • •

Likewise, if others around you are suffering through their own downturns, it's your duty to find the positive out of what they are going through and pick them up. When I was at Pittsburgh with head coach Paul Evans, we had a point guard, Mike Goodson, who led our team in assists during the 1986–87 season. During one particular stretch, Mike was struggling big-time. He'd throw passes into the stands, he couldn't shoot straight, and he had no focus or concentration. He was playing so badly I wanted Coach Evans to try anything to help the kid get back to his comfort zone. So one day I suggested we have Michael Goodson Day at practice.

"What do you mean?" Coach Evans asked me.

"Let's just praise Mike for everything he does today in the gym," I explained. "Anything he does, we say, 'Atta boy, Mike. Great pass.' It doesn't matter if he breaks a guy's nose with the pass, we want to build him up. If he picks up a towel off the gym floor, we'll go into raptures over it. 'Way to bend down, Mike. Great form.'"

Coach agreed, and we made it a point of emphasis for our next practice. You know what? After the first hour of practice, Mike was starting to show more of his usual self. He wasn't trying to make the hard pass. He defended with passion. He started to believe in himself again.

In the intervening years, I've used the method with several of my players. I just tell my coaches, "Today is going to be So-and-So Day. We don't ride him, we heap praise on him, and we see if it brings him out of his funk."

I can't say it always works, but I've had more success than failure with it. Sometimes it's something as simple as having a "Day" for yourself that will change the tide.

The end result when you do this for someone can be something like the letter I received after appearing on the Jim Rome radio show during the 2007–08 season. Again, this was an instance when I knew I had found significance because my message was resonating with others.

It was this note that convinced me once and for all that this book was needed by millions of Americans. Callers to Jim's show and letter and email writers after it let me know my message was one people needed to hear. To me, a letter like this is a "W"—a win. It's that type of feeling you will experience when you help others in any manner of ways.

Dear Mr. Calipari:

[I heard you] on the Jim Rome Show, and the interview that you had with him changed my life in many ways. I was

recently fired from my job that I had planned on developing a long-lasting career [at], with a company I enjoyed working for. There were a few things that were out of my control and [thus] I was let go by the company. This was the hardest thing I have had to go through. I didn't know what to do the next day, and I didn't know how I was going to provide for my family.

I was traveling to another interview and feeling sorry for myself when I turned on the Jim Rome Show and you were talking about the very issue I was going through. At the conclusion of the interview I felt a sense of confidence I thought I had lost. I realized that I was not the only person who has gone through an experience like this. I turned to my family and close friends for support and networking. As you shared a story about how [Charlotte Hornets head coach] Larry Brown helped you through your tough time, I realized how important it is to have good people around you and to help others who may be in need. I wanted to take your advice and reach out to one person a day, and to never give up. To make a long story short, I found my confidence and was able to find a great job I am extremely excited to begin.

Thank you for taking the time to read this letter. Your interview that day changed my attitude in a very positive way. Thank you for sharing your story and I will always be a fan of yours. I wish you the best of luck this year and many years to come.

Sincerely,
Eric Sutterfield
Park City, Utah

Eric needed to know he wasn't alone. He needed to hear there was light at the end of the tunnel. It was so gratifying to know I had helped him, and I started thinking of how many others—especially in these uncertain economic times—I could make an impact on. It gave me an incomparable, satisfying feeling to know I had resonated and connected with people.

Along those lines, I want you to not only hear what I'm saying, but you need to make it your own. As each season evolves, my teams go from just practicing and doing what the coaches say to having good practices and then eventually to having *great* practices. By that time, the players are comfortable in our system and have become aware of what they need to do to make themselves more valuable to the team. They do more than listen; they absorb, adapt, and adjust with confidence and clarity.

I hope that's what you have been able to do while reading this book. We're about to embark on some of the most important work you will do as a member of my team, and it will be your confidence and clarity that decide how successful your bounce back will be.

> **PractiCal Point:** Make everything your own,
> and use each positive step forward to build
> your confidence for the task ahead.

• • •

What you absolutely cannot do at this stage of your bounce back is let your attitude sag. The ability to stay upbeat is something I want to coach you on aggressively. At this point in your bounce back, you want people to see you in a positive and optimistic place. Even if you're having a down day, you want the people you're reaching out to to want to hear from you and help you. Let's say you have a friend named Jim who you have heard through the grapevine is going through a rough patch. Your cell phone rings, and up pops "Call from: Jim" and his phone number. You don't hesitate to answer it because you have always liked Jim and would do anything to help him.

Well, after about fifteen minutes of conversation with Jim, he has hit you with every little brutal detail of his lousy life. He's complained from the word "Hello"; he's denigrated himself, his family, his boss, and just about everyone he ever knew. He blames all those people, the economy, the president, and the media. When you finally get off the call, you realize that he has drained you and sucked the energy out your day.

This happens a few more times until you can't take it anymore. The next time his number shows up on your phone, you hit the "Eat Poop" button, as my daughter Erin so genteelly calls it, and hope he doesn't leave a message. A few minutes later he calls your home or office line. Your spouse or secretary answers and informs you "Jim's on the phone."

You panic. You're looking for any excuse to get out of the call.

No matter how close a friend Jim is, you know there's nothing new you can say to him. There's no getting through to him until he begins to take responsibility for his actions and gets into a better frame of mind. Jim has become the caller ID *nobody* wants to see. You want to avoid him like poison ivy until you know he's ready to be helped.

As your bounce back takes incremental steps, think about Jim—it's one thing to feel frustrated and want to vent, but don't ever let that be the dominant part of the conversation. Don't be the type of person who steals the peace and disrupts the day; **don't be the caller ID no one wants to see.**

Remember, we're in a period of our history that some are calling the "Second Great Depression," and chances are everyone you're in touch with is dealing with some kind of life turmoil. You have to keep that in mind, especially in the course of your bounce back. We tend to magnify our own issues and forget the suffering of others.

The person you do want to become is my aunt Catherine. Everyone has an Aunt Catherine. These are the uplifting people in your life. They are the ones who have always been there for you, regardless of your place in life. More than being there, they have always made you feel good, simply from their words, their gestures, and their aura.

Throughout my life, whenever I needed a little boost—from my teen years all the way through adulthood—I would be sure to visit or talk to Aunt Catherine.

Whenever I was in Moon Township, I'd go to her house, and she'd always greet me with a big hug.

"Here comes my athlete, Johnny," she would boast. "You look so strong."

As a kid, I was 112 pounds soaking wet. I looked like a science-lab skeleton. But every time, without fail, she made me feel special. No matter what was going on in her life, she always made an effort to make the people around her feel loved and respected.

My aunt has since passed away, but even to this day, I still feel the impact she had on me each and every time I saw her. As part of your bounce back, think about how you could have that impact on the people you interact with on a daily basis.

This is just another example of why it's so important to surround yourself with people you can trust to be supportive of you through whatever you're going through. I believed in the people around me, and they believed in me. I've always made it a point to have positive-thinking people around me who will not wilt under the pressure of one bad day, one bad loss, or a streak of several defeats. In my job, we're dealing with the fragile psyches of eighteen-, nineteen- and twentysomething-year-old young men. They look to me and my staff for direction and support—if there are negative people in those positions, the kids will sense it, and it will poison our team. **You want people around you who are able to take issues *off* your plate, not ones who will pile on more.**

If you allow the negative to dominate your thoughts during your bounce back, you, too, will be poisoned. That's not acceptable from my players, and it's not acceptable from you. I believe in you more than you may believe in yourself right now, and until we are equal in that category, you need to heed these words, okay?

Here's how I want you to start your days: Look in the mirror and say, "Everything I'm going to do today will be positive. I'll be upbeat when people talk to me." It sounds like Stuart Smalley on *Saturday Night Live*, I know. But trust me; after you do it for a few days, it will become second nature.

Any negative thoughts that enter your mind, force them out. You can use little sayings if you want, things like "the past is the past" or "look forward, not backward," anything that gives you the visualization of being positive. There are millions of them out there on the internet; find a couple that resonate with you.

Then every night before you go to bed, I want you to reflect on the day and take at least one good thing from every day. It can be something as small as getting to the gym to work out or as large as reconciling a past friendship. You need to accentuate the positive of something you did so that you can go to bed proud.

What will this do for you? Well, first it will show you that not everything sucks, and second, it will teach you that even the smallest of victories can be used as inspiration to get to the next level. When you're first starting out on your bounce back or when you're leading people through a similar situation, it's important to take the positives out of each and every accomplishment. Later on, we will discuss the value of getting "small victories," and the method is truly an effective way to keep progressing.

In no time, you'll notice how your positive attitude changes how people look at you and talk about you. You want to be able to draw people to you, because, at some level, people are going to have to reach out and help you during this process. They won't do that until they feel the positive energy from you. If you stay positive, think positive, and are positive all the time, people will gravitate to you. You know why? Because you make them feel good. They realize they feel bubbly around you, and they seek opportunities to be with you and, when necessary, to help you. **Be a magnet, not a repellent.**

> **PractiCal Point:** Stay upbeat, and don't become the caller ID no one wants to see.

CHAPTER 8

BECOME THE RECRUITER, NOT THE RECRUIT

CREATE YOUR BRAND IDENTITY

ooking back on it, my "first" bounce-back reentry opportunity came very shortly after I was let go by the Nets. About a week later I got a call from Michael Goldberg, the executive director of the NBA Coaches' Association. ESPN had reached out to him to gauge my interest in being an analyst for its ESPN show *NBA Matchup* and some occasional work on ESPN2's *NBA 2Night.* (The opening I would be filling on *Matchup,* ironically enough, was created when Jim Lynam left the show to join the Nets as an assistant. Again, you just never know how things are going to play out!)

I was grateful for the opportunity and jumped at the chance to work with the show's talent, Andre Aldridge and Fred Carter. ESPN, its executives, and its producers had always been great to us at UMass, and that familiarity made it even easier.

Whatever my next move would be, I knew I had to stay fresh in people's minds. My four months with ESPN kept me connected to the game, and it kept me in public view.

In any case your ability to maintain some sense of normalcy

and visibility during your rough stretch will benefit you immensely throughout your bounce back. That's what the ESPN gig did for me. Maybe more than anything, that job opportunity reminded me I still had a lot to offer, be it in broadcasting or coaching or whatever path I chose.

I think the tendency for people going through a major life change is to immediately think they won't get back to the stature they enjoyed before things went south. To me, that doesn't make any sense. You got there once, right? What is stopping you from getting there again? For me, I had to reaffirm that since I was good enough to create magic at UMass, why couldn't I do it again?

The only thing that can possibly stand in your way is your own hesitance or reluctance to reach for the moon. If you're of that mind-set right now, I can't stress enough the need to curtail that way of thinking, to refocus, and to boldly walk into the teeth of your bounce back. Don't let your current circumstance or your own self-doubt limit what you are destined to do.

One way to do that is to think of yourself as the "recruiter," not the "recruit." This applies to not only finding a job but to other types of "searches" as well.

Recruiting is the lifeline of intercollegiate athletics at the Division I level. Whether it's in football, basketball, lacrosse, or any of the revenue-generating sports, the ability to consistently bring elite-level student-athletes onto your campus and into your program is what will ultimately dictate your success or your failure as a college coach. An old saying reminds us, "It's the Jimmys and the Joes, not the Xs and the Os." Great players make even mediocre coaches look like Red Auerbach.

I've been fortunate throughout my career to have some outstanding recruiters on my staffs. From Bruiser Flint, John Robic,

Tony Barbee, and Bill Bayno in the early days at UMass to Steve Roc-caforte, Derek Kellogg, Chuck Martin, Josh Pastner, Rod Strickland, and Orlando Antigua in Memphis and at Kentucky, my assistants have universally been recognized for their tenacity and thoroughness on the recruiting side. It hasn't always been about finding the McDonald's All-Americans like Derrick Rose and Tyreke Evans either. We've prided ourselves on our knack for finding diamonds in the rough and molding those players into professional ballplayers. As we've had more and more success and developed more and more players into pros, recruits have been more open to and intrigued by what we can offer to young men. The style we play has been a big factor as well, as I've learned in our move to Kentucky—kids love the *way* we play and want to learn our system.

I never stop thinking about recruiting, and neither should you. It's all-consuming when it's done right. Our players are required to have one day a week off throughout the season, and that is my recruiting day. Do you know what I did the day after we lost to Kansas in the national title game? I went on the road recruiting, hoping to build on the success we had in reaching that game. It was therapeutic to get right back into the flow of things, be among people, and reassure myself that everything was okay.

You need to start looking around for opportunities that you can seize to get yourself back in the game.

There was a famous game while I was at Pitt where six-foot-six, 230-pound center/man-child Jerome Lane dunked so emphatically at home against Providence that he shattered the backboard. The incomparable Bill Raftery, who was doing play-by-play on the game, let out the now legendary line, "Send it in, Jerome!"

As everyone was going crazy over the dunk and the demolition of the backboard, I ran out on the court and started collecting pieces of the glass backboard and putting them in my pockets. I eventually sent those pieces to various kids we were recruiting. You do anything you can in recruiting to stand out.

> **PractiCal Point:** Prepare yourself to be the impulsion that drives your revitalization forward, and take pride in your ability to control your future.

• • •

It's not enough to *want* to recruit well in my business, and it won't be enough to *want* to find the best reentry point for your bounce back. You need to attack it the way I demand my players pursue loose balls—all out and with no regard for anyone else on the court.

This is why I put a lot of weight on handling recruiting the right way and using all the tools in my toolbox to my advantage. That's exactly what you should be doing as you enter the next phase of your bounce back.

Whether you're looking for a job, a spouse, or a new house, you have to aggressively recruit what you want. Don't sit there and think others are going to come to you and offer you the world. Recruiting is an active pursuit, not a passive one, just like your bounce back.

In recruiting, my toolbox has three major instruments that I consider the most important:

1. Our graduation rate: When we started, the University of Memphis had not graduated a scholarship freshman from 1989 to 1996, according to university records; at the end of the 2008–2009 season, we graduated nineteen of the twenty-

three players who went through our program from 2002 to 2009. When we were at UMass, our graduation rate was right around 80 percent. I will continue to emphasize this at Kentucky. Numbers don't lie, and those numbers speak volumes about our priorities.

2. Developing young men: It's very rare that a young man who comes in as a freshman in our system remains the baby-faced boy he presents in his initial team photo. We put an emphasis not only on developing players on the court but also on forming them into men off it. The guys who don't go pro are given every tool necessary to succeed in whatever line of business they enter. We teach both life skills and basketball skills.

3. Developing pros: Statistics tell us that the percentage of college players who go on to long and prosperous NBA careers is fairly small. But we've had great success in developing potential pros into NBA-ready players. Beyond that, we've placed any number of guys in professional leagues overseas. The cornerstones of my UMass program—players like Harper Williams, Lou Roe, and Jim McCoy—have all enjoyed prosperous careers in various countries. Those are guys who didn't come in as McDonald's All-Americans, but who invested in our coaching and instruction and ultimately made themselves a lot of money.

When I am recruiting a prospective student-athlete to play for me, I consider the first five minutes after meeting the young man to be the most critical part of the process. I want to be sure I can instantly gain the youngster's trust and that of his parent or guardian. I will not make promises I can't keep, and I won't guarantee playing time or a position in the NBA. If anyone is doing that, I'd venture to guess he's either lying or desperate or both.

Instead, in those first five minutes I am able to listen to the young man and get a picture of what his dreams and aspirations are. I take notes. I want to listen to the way the young man communicates with me, the questions he asks, and the demeanor he presents. I've been doing this long enough to know within those first five or ten minutes whether the recruit will or won't fit into our program. I say this to impress upon you the importance of always having your own game face on. You never know who's paying attention, you never know who might be able to offer you a break, so you have to behave as if every situation is an opportunity to make something good happen for yourself.

Let me give you an example from a memorable recruiting visit Bruiser Flint took me on when we were at UMass. Bruiser was pretty high on the kid, and I always trust my assistants' evaluations. We walked into the young man's house, met him and his mother, and sat down for a discussion. Literally, within the first five minutes the kid disrespected his mother in front of us. Just some rude, childish stuff, but it caught my attention right away. I looked at Bruiser, and he could tell I wasn't happy about the kid's behavior. We finished up quickly, said good-bye to the kid and his mom, and got into our rental car twenty minutes later.

"Bru," I said. "You know I always respect what you do on the recruiting trail, and there are very few better at it than you, but —"

"I know, Cal," Bru interrupted, "You didn't like the way he treated his mom."

"That's right," I said. "You didn't know this kid well enough to bring me into his home. If he's not respecting his mom in their own home, how will he respect me?"

Bru knew exactly what I meant. It's something he's carried with him to Drexel University, and it's part of the reason he and his staff have been so successful in the always-tough Colonial Athletic Association (the league that the Final Four Cinderella of all time, George Mason, plays in).

That's why listening and observing during your bounce back are more important than talking. We can discover so much about people just by listening, and I encourage you to listen much more than you speak as you go through this process.

A great place to start your own personal "listening tour" is with your former employer, supervisor, or coworkers. If you're involved in the dissolution of a relationship but still on good terms with your ex, by all means try and have an honest, heart-to-heart discussion in order to get a grasp on what it is that may have led to your breakup. Keep in mind, however, that partnerships of any kind don't fail for one specific reason. There is always a combination of factors, and you cannot allow yourself to take all the blame. That's just not healthy, and it's just not reality, I assure you.

Once you have been able to self-assess and recognize the culmination of moments that have led to this point in your life, you are ready to go ask for assessment from people you worked with or who were involved in the trigger event.

In the instance of job loss, career coach Bobbie LaPorte suggests reaching out to your ex-boss or supervisor. "Have them tell you what happened and what led to the decision," Bobbie told me. "Ask them what you did wrong, what you could have done better, and at what stage you started losing their faith or trust.

"That will help to fill in some of the blanks about what led to where you are," she said. "There may have been things you were doing that you don't even realize you were doing, and to get those things out in the open will only be beneficial down the road."

Let me tell you a few of the people I went back and talked to. There were people within the organization I was still in touch with, and I made it a point to reach out to them to see what they felt some of my failings were. I was able to talk to players I coached and players I coached against, and I was also able to tap into other observers of the NBA whom I trusted and respected. I sought honest feedback from coaches I coached against and general managers I dealt with.

In fact, my very first interview for ESPN's *NBA Matchup* was with late Hall of Famer Chuck Daly, who was the head coach of the Orlando Magic at the time. Chuck had coached in New Jersey in the early 1990s, so he knew all too well what a challenging job it was. He was great to listen to and was brutally honest with me about everything, from the way I coached on the sideline to the personnel decisions I made.

You can't be afraid or ashamed to ask for an honest evaluation of how they saw your downfall unfold. By listening to others, we are able to see things we otherwise might not have noticed ourselves.

PractiCal Point: Get feedback from people who were around you when your fall was taking place.

• • •

Once the NBA season finished in June of 1999, I finally got a chance to *really* catch my breath. The ESPN gig was finished, and the "silly season" in college basketball was also completed. That's the time of year, usually in March and April, when college coaches get hired and fired. In fact, if you ever go to the Final Four and hang out in the designated coaches' hotel for any amount of time, you will see the biggest sideshow of Final Four week is the coaching rumor mill. That year alone, my name was associated with jobs at Notre Dame, Michigan, Pittsburgh, and Georgia.

Even though I had some interest in a couple of different jobs, I didn't think there was one particular job that was the right fit for me. So I cooled my heels for a bit.

That is until Larry Brown called me one day during the summer. Coach Brown was the most important friend I had during those rough times after the Nets fired me. At the time, he was the head coach of the Philadelphia 76ers. In fact, two seasons after my Nets firing, Coach Brown guided the 2000–01 Philly team to the NBA Finals for the first time in eighteen years. The following year, he was inducted into the Naismith Basketball Hall of Fame based on a storied career that has seen over one thousand professional wins and successful coaching stops at two of the most storied college basketball programs of all time, UCLA and Kansas. He remains the only coach to win both an NCAA title and an NBA title.

Coach was always more than a friend; he was my mentor ever since I worked for him at the University of Kansas as an unpaid assistant. During that stretch after my firing we were talking four or five times a week, which is something that continues to this day even as Coach Brown has reentered the NBA in 2008–09 as the head coach of the Charlotte Bobcats.

(Coach had actually offered me a job with him the day after I got fired. He told me I could come with him to the 76ers if I wanted. "It's sad what happened to you, John," he told me at the time. "It's real unfair, but that's the way it goes. Come with me, and I'll find something for you to do." I thought about it, but decided the best thing for me was to get away from coaching for a bit. Let that be another lesson: don't make a knee-jerk decision when you're in the beginning of your bounce back. You've got to take your time and make rational decisions that will be good for you in the long run rather than grabbing at the first thing that comes your way.)

Coach initiated many calls just to check in and see how I was doing in the first few weeks of my bounce back. We would talk about all sorts of things, from basketball to our families and especially about my future. I remember him repeating his offer to me at one point after the first couple of months had passed. "John, if something doesn't happen for you at the end of the year, I want you to come work for me," he said.

I appreciated his words and took his offer to mean that I could do scouting for the 76ers or maybe serve as a consultant to Coach and the team. I kept it in the back of my mind as I pursued some other things, including making a return to television in some capacity.

But after a few more phone calls where Coach reminded me of his offer, I said to him, "Coach, I'm not sure if I want to scout right now, and I—"

"Scout?" Coach Brown interrupted. "Who said anything about scouting? I want you on the bench with me for this upcoming [1999–2000] season. I really need your help, John. Please think about it."

I was blown away. There was no way he "needed me" as much as he claimed. The guy's won more than a thousand pro games, and he's telling me he needs me? Come on.

But he wouldn't stop insisting, and the prospect of being back on an NBA bench was something that really intrigued me. I'm not sure I totally realized it at the time, but Coach Brown was saying he needed me when all along he knew I needed him. I needed to get back into my comfort zone, and Coach Brown wanted to be the one who put me there. (It was gratifying a couple of years later when I was at Memphis and Bruiser Flint was fired by UMass and I could do a similar thing for my good friend. I called Bru immediately and said, "I got you, Bru. If nothing happens for you, you're coming with me." I know Bruiser appreciated that even though there was no doubt he was going to bounce back quickly. Schools were already clamoring for him soon after he was let go at UMass.)

There were a lot of things that appealed to me about joining Coach Brown's staff in Philadelphia, but the biggest drawback was that I would have to spend a lot of time away from my family, as I would need to get a condo in Philadelphia. There was no way we were going to move the family from New Jersey, so Ellen and I discussed the opportunity long and hard before I committed to Coach Brown. In the end, Ellen and I agreed that although it would be a hardship on the kids and on her, it was really the best thing for us all in the long run. It didn't make sense to uproot the family for something that might not be permanent, so we decided to make it work for a year or so.

For your bounce back to be successful, it's so essential that your family is willing to endure some of the inconveniences and realize the short-term hassles will eventually lead to long-term happiness. Ellen was remarkable about all of that—she always has been. A coach's family has to make all kinds of sacrifices, and Ellen and the kids have always done so without complaint, and for that I am always grateful.

When the news of my going with Coach Brown began to seep out, a lot of people asked if I was going to have a problem being an assistant again after eleven years of being a head coach (eight at UMass and three with the Nets). But I didn't see it that way at all. I was just excited about coaching again, period. I was an assistant before I was a head coach, and I truly just wanted to do anything I could to help Coach Brown and the Philadelphia organization.

I valued the opportunity to work with the 76ers players, especially Allen Iverson, whom I've always considered a special talent. My point is that a change of title doesn't matter when you feel like you have a great opportunity. If an offer comes your way that you're excited about, you cannot let pride hold you back from it.

For me, there was also the bonus of the fact I'd be able to coach alongside the man who had given me my first college coaching job at the age of twenty-three in 1982. I started with Coach at Kansas, and now I was getting the chance not only to be reintroduced to him, but also to see what kind of evolution he had gone through since we last shared bench space. I knew I would be able to learn so much from him, the way I had almost twenty years prior.

The other thing latching on with Coach Brown did for me was give me someone to "defend my honor." The Nets were being pretty nasty after our separation, and when they continued to lose under the coach who replaced me, I became the target of their frustration and anger.

But for me to try and defend myself would have been futile. Coach Brown, however, thought he was just the man to come to my defense. He did it with both his words and his actions.

"I've been with some great ones, but I think John's the whole package," Coach Brown said at the time I was hired. "It really bugged me that certain people say he failed in New Jersey last year. New Jersey doesn't have all great character guys. They didn't have an assistant coach who was loyal to him, or a GM who was loyal to him, or a president who wanted to see him succeed. Don Casey, John Nash, and Michael Rowe got to the new owners and killed him. And that's a fact. They all stuck him right in the back. The players who really mattered cared about him, not the Jayson Williamses of the world.

Williams and Kendall Gill are the only two guys he had problems with, and everybody who has coached those guys has had a problem with them. Bottom line."

I certainly didn't want Coach to say those words, and when he did, it sort of put the spotlight back on me for a little bit. But as he said to me, "It is the only way they will stop what they're saying about you, John. When they speak now, they will be guarded." As usual, Coach was right, because no one from the Nets organization was as quick to bash me after that.

We all need advocates in our lives and especially in our bounce backs—those people in the professional realm or within our own social circles—who will not let rumors spread and who will not let misconceptions be perpetuated.

Still, for good measure, Coach Brown—who I should note was also once fired by the Nets back in 1983—also had another trick up his sleeve. He maintains to this day he did not orchestrate what occurred on November 20, 1999, when the 76ers visited the 1–8 Nets for a game at the Meadowlands.

In that game, Coach Brown got ejected at the tail end of the first quarter for arguing a call with referee Marc Davis. He left me to run the team for the rest of the game. We wound up winning 100–96, and the Philadelphia players gave me a hero's welcome in the locker room after the game. They presented me with the game ball, which the Nets management demanded back! No kidding.

For his part, Coach Brown told the media after the contest, "I didn't say anything that warranted being thrown out. I wouldn't have left [John] in a situation like that. That's the last thing I'd do to him. I put him in a tough position."

He sure did, but I know he did it with the best of intentions—

even if he still won't admit it. But this is what can happen when you keep the people you depend on most close to you; they'll give back to you in ways you could never imagine!

That season with Coach Brown and his staff of Randy Ayers, Maurice Cheeks, and John Kuester was the greatest seven months of my professional life, and I mean that sincerely. I'm eternally grateful for what Coach did for me and how comfortable the assistants made me feel. He made it seem like he needed me and that he couldn't be as effective without me. That was an incredibly generous and inspiring thing to have happen, and it's just the kind of jump start I needed to really put my bounce back into overdrive.

I'm guessing there's someone like Coach Brown in your life who is just waiting to help you. Not everyone, however, will make the first move. Sometimes you have to reach out first and set things in motion. I guarantee you when it does happen, it will be like a whole new world of opportunity opening up for you.

You won't fly high in one step, but once you get a little momentum going, your opportunity to soar will be there for you.

> **PractiCal Point:** Allow others to help you,
> reach out to them, and don't be too
> proud to accept their offers.

• • •

Whether or not you are able to find someone willing to give you that opportunity to jump-start your bounce back, there are certain things you need to be doing on a daily basis at this point.

I would say first and foremost you need to market yourself. That's probably a lot easier to understand if your bounce back is centered on a job search, but don't think it can't be beneficial for whatever rejuvenation you're going through. I was a marketing major at Clarion State (now Clarion University) in Pennsylvania, so you need to understand that I look at almost everything as a marketing opportunity. Believe me, it has helped immeasurably as I've rebuilt broken "franchises."

If you were involved in a failed relationship and you are now ready to get back out there, it's important you let your friends, relatives, and coworkers know that you would like to start dating or meeting new people. Let them know what your intentions are and how you want to proceed. There's an entire industry that has grown from trying to find people their true loves, and you can begin to use any of those legitimate, proven websites or services.

You truly have to keep yourself open to any and all opportunities. You just never know. My dad would tell me growing up, "You dream it, you say it, you talk about it, and someone will come knocking at your door with it."

Here's a good example of that very credo in practice:

When I was a student at Clarion (I had transferred there after two years at UNC Wilmington), my roommate, Marty Tougher, and I had moved off campus into a two-bedroom mobile home right next to the gym. We thought we were it—we had our own pad, we were right next to the gym, and we were saving a bit of money from what we would have paid in the dorms. Life was good.

One night we were sitting around, and I started to run the numbers of what we were paying the landlord in monthly rent. I was like, "Marty, this trailer doesn't cost as much as we pay in one year to live in it."

He said, "Yeah, you're right."

So my next thought was, "I want to buy a trailer, and I'll rent it out, and we'll pay for our rent with it."

Marty was all for it, but it became my obsession. Everywhere I was, whomever we met, I'd talk about wanting to buy a trailer. That was what I wanted to do, and I wasn't going to stop until I had one. Everyone would look at me like I had three heads. "You're a college student; what do you want a trailer for?" they'd laugh.

But I wanted it. I saw it as an investment.

So one day, we're hanging out in the trailer, and there's a knock at the door. It was Ilene, who lived in the trailer next door.

"I hear you're looking for a trailer," she said. "A friend of mine in Frogtown has three he's looking to sell."

Frogtown was about ten miles south of Clarion on Route 66, and I'm thinking, *It's Frogtown—how expensive can a trailer in Frogtown be?*

I drove down, checked out the trailers, and bought one. There was an open spot in the trailer park we were living in, so I got it, put the trailer up on blocks, balanced it, skirted it, the whole deal. (I can't lie, my dad had to help me!) It was great, and Dad was right—I dreamt it, I thought it, and wouldn't you know—knock, knock—it happened! I wound up buying another one that I lived in for a year. I had to borrow some money from my dad to pay for them both, but I rented out the two-bedroom to some girls from school and paid my dad back within six months.

When I graduated and was at Kansas making no money at all, my sole income was the rent from those trailers. After I left Kansas, I sold the really nice trailer for twice as much as I paid for both trailers originally, and I donated the other one to Clarion State as a write-off.

I guess it was my introduction into the world of real estate, but for me it was a marketing opportunity. That's the way you need to think of your bounce back.

> **PractiCal Point:** Dream it, say it, talk about it, and someone will come knocking at your door.

. . .

Let me share another great story with you. It's one I tell people all the time because it perfectly illustrates why you always have to be alert to your surroundings and be willing to give your bounce back a kick start.

You should recognize the name Jerry Colangelo as both a Naismith Basketball Hall of Famer and the man who oversaw Team USA's basketball resurgence which led to a stirring gold medal in the Beijing 2008 Summer Olympics.

I've known Jerry for years and have always respected his work ethic and his dedication to the game of basketball. Jerry is one of the most knowledgeable basketball minds we have in our game. Incredibly, he almost never got the chance to prove it.

After two years (1960–62) at the University of Illinois, where he earned All-Big Ten honors and captained the basketball team, Jerry began a business, renting tuxedoes in his hometown of Chicago. As he tells it, Jerry poured his heart and soul into the business, but after three years he had no choice but to admit his venture was a failure. In 1965 at the age of twenty-six, Jerry had just about no money and fewer options. He was playing semipro basketball for $50 a night and struggling to find a better life for him and his wife.

One day, he found himself sitting at his kitchen table, cleaning out his wallet. Among the slips of paper and tattered receipts was a business card with the name Dick Klein on it. Jerry couldn't quite remember who Klein was. He thought long and hard on where he may have gotten the card, and finally he remembered his father-in-law handing it to him about two years prior. "You should meet this guy," his father-in-law said at the time. Jerry never had the time because he was so obsessed with making his tux-rental business fly.

Now, with very little else to occupy his time, he figured it was time to give Mr. Klein a call. He called and introduced himself, and Klein asked Jerry to come into his Chicago office for an informal discussion—basically an informational interview.

Klein ran a one-man merchandising operation, and at the time Jerry came in, Klein was overwhelmed by the demands of his customers. After meeting and talking for a bit, the two hit it off, and Klein asked Jerry to come work with him. Jerry quickly accepted.

As the two grew closer and spent long hours together, Jerry discovered Klein's real dream and passion was to bring a professional basketball franchise to Chicago. It would be no easy task, but Klein pursued it, and Jerry was a sponge in observing and helping with Klein's quest. By 1966, Klein succeeded in landing a Chicago franchise from the NBA. Jerry had been with Klein from the start of the process and stayed on with him as the Chicago Bulls began play. By his second year with Klein and the Bulls, the NBA expanded out west, and when the Phoenix franchise was awarded, Jerry was in demand because of his background with the start-up Bulls. Jerry was offered and took the Phoenix Suns general manager job in 1968.

He eventually bought the team and built the Suns into a championship team and in the process became legendary for his resourceful-ness and ingenuity in the city of Phoenix. When baseball expanded to the city in 1998, it was Jerry who was the franchise's managing partner and owner. He brought a number of pro sports franchises to the city and simultaneously grew his reputation as one of the nation's most knowledgeable sports minds.

When USA Basketball needed someone to restore the glory to Team USA after it had fallen behind some of its international compe-tition in the early part of this century, they turned to Jerry as its man-aging director of the USA Basketball Men's Senior National Team program.

Think about it. Jerry Colangelo went from a failed tuxedo renter to the king of USA Basketball and one of the great success stories in all of sports. And you know how he did it? He kept all his options open, including the one that fell out of his wallet onto a kitchen table. I love that story. Jerry took one informational-type sit-down with a businessman and parlayed it into a brand-new career that carried him into the Hall of Fame.

There is a story like that waiting inside you, and it's time to bring it out. As you bring it out, there is a simple approach I want you to employ if you haven't already been doing it. Show your best side at *all* times. Allow that side to be seen by everyone, not just a select few.

I don't care if you're filling the car with gas, standing in the check-out line at the grocery store, or on a first date. You need to constantly be presenting the best you possible, and that begins with maintaining the upbeat, positive attitude that I have coached you on throughout this book.

> **PractiCal Point:** Be open to every opportunity,
> and view everyone you meet as a potential
> character in your bounce-back story.

• • •

This is also the time in your rebirth where you want to rediscover the "swagger" you had prior to your trigger event. I guarantee you had some form of swagger and it's time to cultivate it again. What is swagger, you ask? Swagger is something I strive to develop with each and every one of my teams. I think we all have swaggerability in us; it's just a matter of tapping into it.

The word itself has become sort of trendy in sports circles in recent years; it seems like every team that is on a winning streak or playing really well all of a sudden has a "swagger" about them.

But to me, swagger is much more than that. It's not necessarily born solely from winning—although that certainly helps. I want my teams—and *you*—to be confident to the point where the other team (or prospective employer) *feels* it. I do not want you to be arrogant or cocky; that's not what swagger is about.

With arrogance comes sloppy, selfish play, but with swagger comes domination. Swagger is built when you've really worked hard, invested in your purpose, and prepared for whatever you are walking into. It is the confidence you have that shows you know you have the energy and enthusiasm to face any challenge in order to reach your goal. You can't fake a swagger. Swagger is developed and nurtured over time, and even then it only truly emerges when you believe that things are going to go your way.

When we were at Memphis, our program got on an unprecedented conference winning streak that stretched over three seasons,
beginning in 2006. Through each and every one of those games,
we carried a swagger into the arena with us. When it gets down to
crunch time, my team knows we're going to win the game *and* the
other team knows we're going to win the game as well. They feel,
see, and are intimidated by our swagger. I think my team's swagger
is based mostly on our defense, which is something I have instilled
in every college team I've coached. We take great pride in being able
to stop the other team from scoring. When we defend for a full shot
clock and force the opponent into a thirty-five-second clock violation, that lifts our entire team, because we know all five of the guys on
the floor did their job to perfection. It's a wonderful energizer for the
entire team.

The swagger that I'm talking about is based on a "Refuse to Lose"
attitude that became a popular rallying cry when I was at UMass. (It
was also the title of my first book with my dear friend Dick "Hoops"
Weiss.)

"Refuse to Lose" (RTL) doesn't mean you are going to win every
game, but it does mean you will compete your hardest until the final
horn sounds. When you develop your RTL attitude, it creates within
you a sense of inevitability where you begin to look around and say,
"I deserve good things to happen because I've worked too hard, sacri-
ficed too much, and cared too much to stop now."

I really think that RTL is part of the essence of anyone's bounce
back—you never stop learning, you never stop trying, and you seek
continuous improvement in all areas. Simply put, you Refuse to
Lose.

> **PractiCal Point:** Rediscover your own swagger, put it forth, but don't let it become cocky arrogance.

• • •

Whether you have found that swagger yet or are still striving toward it, I want you to also begin thinking about marketing yourself. This can be done in a number of ways, many of which are available to you on the internet. I don't claim to be a computer geek, but I've surfed around the Web enough to know there are reputable business- and social-networking sites that have become essential tools for people trying to find work or career advancement.

"Web sites like LinkedIn, Plaxo, and even Facebook or MySpace are very active these days and are especially helpful to people," career coach Bobbie LaPorte said. "They are a formal mechanism that employers can use to identify qualified candidates for open positions."

That said, Bobbie emphasized to me the importance of making sure your own pages are professional looking and convey the type of employee you can be. Your résumé needs to be flawless, up-to-date, and organized before you post it at websites like Monster.com or Careerbuilder.com.

"I actually suggest people start with their natural network of people they know well and with whom they can be honest and up-front," Bobbie said. "You want people who can credibly represent you and refer you to possible employers. You start with that, and from there, if you're clear about what you want to do, you ask those people to refer you and help you network *into* companies. That way your network expands from the initial point. But again, you've got to be clear in what you want so others can help you. If your vision isn't clear, then your network of helpers can't be clear when they are talking you up to friends, colleagues, and other executives."

This speaks directly to your own personal marketing plan. I'll give you an example of how I branded the Memphis Tigers basketball program when I was there, and hopefully it will give you some ideas of what your own brand identity can be. This is exactly what I told my team as we entered the heart of our 2008–09 season.

I want the brand of any team I coach to be one that other teams get inspired to play against. Beating our brand means something to every opponent we face, and we despise giving them that satisfaction.

My programs have built this reputation over the years based on these four principles:

1. We play viciously, in the best sense of the word. We are in your face defending on each and every possession. We play like every moment counts.

2. We play with toughness. If there's a loose ball, we're diving for it. If there's a rebound up for grabs, we're scrapping, banging, and pursuing that ball with unbridled passion so that we can walk away from the court knowing that we didn't let a single opportunity slip by. We're a physically tough, grind-it-out team with swagger but mentally tough enough to be composed.

3. We play fast but in control. *Real* fast. Teams know we will run from the opening tip to the final horn, and if they can't keep up with our pace, they will be run out of the gym. We never lose sight of the goal, which is winning.

4. We play unselfishly. Our players look for open team-mates and take as much pride in an assist as they do in scoring. We're always trying to get at least five guys to score ten or more points.

Now, preaching about those four tenets is one thing. But our true brand identity comes when each and every member of the team feels a responsibility to live up to those standards every play of every game. They must take pride in representing the brand and have passion for continuing the legacy that has been established by players who came before them. They "own" the house, the furnishings, the fixtures, the bricks, and the mortar that make up our program.

Antonio Anderson was a junior on our Final Four team and was one of the most earnest, hardworking, and respectful young men I have ever been around. Every year he improved, and every year he did everything we asked of him and more. He's from Lynn, Massachusetts, just outside of Boston, and his brother Anthony was recruited by Bruiser Flint and played at UMass. They come from a really close-knit family with great morals and perspective.

As a senior, Antonio became the unquestioned leader of our team, and at one point early in the 2008–09 season, we were talking about the difference from the prior year's team.

"Coach, if one of us went to the mall or the movies last year, all thirteen of us went," Antonio said. "It was like we were brothers, just with different mothers."

But through December 2008, our team was like a bunch of orphans. I leaned on Antonio to impress upon our guys how important it is to be best friends and to share in one another's success.

When I'd try and do it, Antonio would stop and correct me if I said the Final Four team "really liked each other."

"Coach," he'd say, "we loved each other."

After we started 6–3, Antonio made it his mission to instill that love and create that type of bond within the new mixture of players we were working into our family.

Simply, Antonio would say, "That's how we do it here at Memphis. We all get along, we all care for one another, and if you don't want to be a part of that, then pack your bags."

He forced our guys to own their performances and to understand that what's good for any individual on our team is good for the entire team.

Antonio, maybe more than any player we've had, knew exactly what our brand identity was.

Do you know what yours is?

> **PractiCal Point:** Decide what you want your brand identity to be, and then own it.

PRACTICE PLAN: #4

CREATE YOUR BRAND IDENTITY:

EMPHASIS OF THE DAY: Create the "Final Four" aspects of your brand identity, and live to that brand.

This is an exercise I see you doing as an individual workout first and then as a team workout with your Kitchen Cabinet and/or other close advisors and supporters.

I use individual workouts with our players all the time. Basically, the young man comes to the gym sixty or ninety minutes before we are scheduled to practice, and I focus on a couple of key areas that either need developing, improving, or overhauling. The real true pros feed off being challenged and being asked to improve through one-on-one instruction. You need to adopt that desire and be the sponge players like Derrick Rose, Tyreke Evans, Allen Iverson (in Philadelphia), and Marcus Camby were with me.

These sessions are some of my favorite moments on the practice court—when I am able to teach one-on-one or one-on-two and really help my players continue to make strides in every area of their game.

PURPOSE

I want you to dedicate some time to creating your own brand. First, I'd ask you to think about some of the most successful brand names in your everyday life—brands like Coca-Cola, Nike,

Apple, or Google. When you hear or see those names, you immediately have a picture in your head. For example, when you see the Nike Swoosh, you probably think of the slogan "Just Do It," and then maybe you think of Michael Jordan (who is a brand unto himself), which will lead you to Phil Knight, the founder of the company.

Whatever it is that Swoosh symbolizes to you, I guarantee it spurs an instantaneous vision of one of the world's most recognizable brands. That visceral response has been built over the years every time you see a new ad, a new commercial, or even just somebody walking down the street with it on his shoes. Your brand—even though you may not realize it—has also been building through the course of your life and career.

Now is the time to assess those characteristics that define your brand and get them organized in a way that will allow you to market yourself.

DRILL

Think about your strengths, your assets, and your position in the marketplace. Try and express who you are and what you have to offer with words similar to the boldface ones in my description (below).

I think it will be helpful for you to get a glimpse of what I considered my brand to be before I took the Nets job, after I was fired, and now as I enter my first season at the University of Kentucky. Use these samples to help in creating your own brand identity for your bounce back and beyond. Keep in mind that your brand, like your bounce back, is a living entity. As such, it can change and adapt to the surroundings you find yourself in—let's just make sure you don't make an ill-advised modification like the New Coke gaffe! There's nothing wrong with being the "Classic" brand you have cultivated.

WATCH ME FIRST

My brand when the Nets hired me in 1996:

- **Strong** leader with great interpersonal skills
- **Passionate,** enthusiastic, and dedicated
- Demands **unselfish** play from his players
- **Wins** championships, excels in postseason

By the time the Nets had fired me, those touchstones were all turned upside down, and my strengths all of a sudden felt like they had become weaknesses. I felt like my brand had changed because of all the gossip and bad press; that might have been true to some extent, but my confidence had been shaken, and that led me to doubt my brand too.

My brand when the Nets fired me in 1999:

- Control freak who doesn't play well with others
- Too much of a college, rah-rah guy
- Doesn't allow team to be "star-driven" enough
- Questionable coaching ability

I had to make a conscious effort to shake off those labels and not let them be associated with my new, improved brand as I pursued my next coaching opportunity. I knew—and you must also realize—I was the same guy who, three years earlier, had been given the amazing opportunity to run an NBA ball club.

For me, it meant getting back to the core beliefs I relied on while working my way through all of the jobs and situations that had brought me to the job with the Nets. I had to take back control of the marketing and remind people that the only things different about me were my outlook and my experience pool.

My brand as I began to explore new opportunities:

- A leader with a **vision,** compassion, and perspective

- Graduates his players and **creates opportunities** for them after they leave campus

- Affects others in a positive way—a **role model,** a mentor

- **Motivates** teams to improve throughout the course of every season

- **Empowers** staff and players

This brand definition was how I decided I'd market myself with college administrators. It was also what I wanted my Kitchen Cabinet to be using when they were talking me up to decision makers. Now, start writing down all of the things you want to define your brand. Cull through them and pick the top four that are the most important to you. Once you have developed your own "Final Four" brand identity, be sure to share it with your Kitchen Cabinet and allow them to offer input and tweaks to it.

CHAPTER 9

LET OPPORTUNITY KNOCK

DON'T SETTLE, BUT
DON'T FEAR REINVENTION EITHER

Let's take a minute and look where we are in your bounce back, and while we are doing this, try and focus on how far you have come and how strong and resilient you have been. These dozen items have now positioned you to take back control and find whatever it is that this next chapter in your life will be about:

1. Your trigger event occurred, and your world was thrown out of whack.

2. You tended to your family and took care of those who are most precious to you.

3. You took time to reflect and assess what happened, and you acknowledged there will be several stages to your bounce back.

4. You identified your Kitchen Cabinet and pinpointed what each of those members would "specialize" in during your bounce back.

5. You fought back the demons of the negative thoughts

and focused on being positive, upbeat, and sturdy. You got out from "under the covers."

6. You created a regular routine for yourself and worked toward being happy; you established healthy, productive habits; you rediscovered the goodness you possess and always have possessed.

7. You embraced the concept of "NEXT" and resisted the urges to dwell on your past failings or missteps.

8. You defined what your own success would be made up of and began to seriously consider how you were going to get to that place.

9. You found significance through outside interests and causes.

10. You began to dream and envision your own success once again.

11. You organized your wish list and sought, listened to, and balanced the opinions of others beyond your Kitchen Cabinet.

12. You began to find your "swagger" and market yourself.

Those significant steps bring us to this pivotal moment in your bounce back where you are ready to seek and pursue your reentry opportunity, which will signify the start of the final stage of your bounce back. You now know what you are fleeing from, but it's time to determine where you are going.

I'd love to tell you you're through the worst of it, but coaches, above all, need to be forthright and communicative with their players. The ensuing stages—especially in the uncertain economy of the first decade of this century—will demand that you be as committed and pliant as you've been to battle through to this point. As your coach, it's only fair I warn you of the ambiguous nature of landing a next job, beginning a new relationship, or embarking on a new life's journey. The pursuit of self-satisfaction and enjoyment is much like the pursuit of a championship. It doesn't come about after a week or two of preparation and commitment. Every major accomplishment I have been a part of at UMass, New Jersey, and Memphis has been the result of constant, steady improvement and maturation over the course of months, seasons, and years.

There is no quick fix, no magic wand. But you already know that. I just need you to keep the same positive and upbeat outlook you have given to our team so far. I ask my teams to work until exhaustion and then fight through that fatigue and find an inner strength they may not have known they possessed. **Pain, I need them to understand, kills pain.**

You can do everything to the best of your ability and with the most honest of intentions, but sometimes events just do not unfold the way you had hoped. In other words, you're going to swing and miss a few times. But you cannot take it personally or let that derail your ambitions. A major contributing factor to your bounce back is going to be luck. The fickle nature of the national and international markets over the past few years is affecting everyone and everything, be it business issues or personal concerns. Over the course of writing this book, the unemployment rate has skyrocketed, and with it the time spent unemployed has also grown. Where recent years had seen most people who lost their jobs find new employment within three months, that duration has been creeping closer to five months, and in some industries it could be double that.

You know what? All those indicators only reinforce the message I've been conveying: you are not alone. Millions of Americans are going through turmoil, but the fortunate thing for you is, you chose to seek guidance through this book. I grew up in a blue-collar setting, and the memories I have are of Americans fighting through all kinds of unimaginable setbacks in pursuit of the American Dream.

My grandparents came through Ellis Island to pursue their dreams and make a better life for their children and their children's children. Those dreams led to my grandpa John's dying of black lung when he was fifty-eight, but those dreams also led to my parents' surviving the first Great Depression and raising three, college-educated children who provide them endless hours of joy and happiness, much of it through their eight grandchildren. My parents were high school educated, and they only wanted to have the means by which they could allow me and my two sisters to attend college and have opportunities they only dreamed of. We lived Friday to Friday—that was payday for my dad. When he got paid, we'd take the money, go to the grocery store, and stock up on what we needed to get through the week. There was never much left over. But we didn't know anyone who lived differently, so it was just the way we lived.

You know what? They did it. It wasn't easy, but they—and millions of other Americans—fought, persevered, and came out on the other side stronger and more appreciative than any generation before or since.

That's exactly what we are all going to do in the face of these worrisome times.

For you, that pursuit can be as rewarding and triumphant as you make it. You just need to believe and stick with the principles that have brought you to this point in your bounce back. I read something in psychotherapist Susan Anderson's book *The Journey from Heartbreak to Connection* that fits perfectly with what we are discussing: "Almost anything is bearable if we know it is temporary," Anderson writes.

Realize the truth in those words, and understand your current situation will not last forever. We won't allow it to do so.

> **PractiCal Point:** Recognize that you have achieved incredible results in your bounce back, but that doesn't mean there won't be hitches and impediments. Fight through them with fervor.

• • •

Before I start coaching you in the approach you will take to obtain whatever goal it is you are working toward—be it a job, a new partner, a new home, or simply a new beginning—we need to first agree on how we will characterize victory in your pursuit.

This is important because bounce backs are not always going to conclude with perfectly ideal situations. By no means will you have to settle or just make do, but you do need to recognize that you may need to take what feels like a step back in order to ultimately move forward. Logic dictates many of you will need to accept a lesser job and find a way to work up the corporate ladder from within, rather than being hired at a pay rate commensurate with your previous job. It's possible that there will not be much wiggle room, and in some cases you will be best served by taking whatever offer comes your way, including opportunities you might not have considered previously.

Don't let anyone tell you there's anything wrong with this. A significant part of your bounce back is putting yourself in the best possible situation and then using it as a springboard to complete your story down the road. As long as you are willing to work and give maximum effort to everything you do, the acceptance of a position that is "beneath" you will only be temporary, because you are going to stand out from everyone else with your work ethic.

Think about this one: When I started out in coaching at the age of twenty-three, I was a volunteer assistant at the University of Kansas. Do you know where a volunteer assistant rates on the food chain? Nowhere. He's not on it.

I had no salary at all. None. No benefits. My first bed was a cot that had been used in the movie *The Day After* with Jason Robards and John Lithgow, which was filmed on campus. They used Allen Fieldhouse in the refugee-camp scene, and after they were done filming, they were throwing the cots away. I didn't have a bed, and I couldn't afford one, so I went over and took one of those cots—I got one of the wide suckers. I had to put a piece of plywood under it to protect my back, but that was my first bed in coaching!

You know how I ate? I worked training meals every day. I was the "peas or corn?" guy.

"What would you like? Peas? Hey, I'll be there early for practice if you want to do some extra shooting," I'd say to the players. Next guy comes up: "What would you like, peas or corn? I'll be in the gym early if you want to get extra work in." That's what I did.

I did anything and everything. I had no life—I was too old to hang out with the students and too poor to hang out with the coaches, so I just got into basketball. I went out there with two pairs of shoes, three pairs of slacks, a blue blazer, three shirts, and two ties. And guess what? I was happy as hell because I was doing exactly what I wanted to be doing.

Now, I'm not trying to give you one of those "I walked up and down a hill barefoot in three feet of snow" deals, but this is where I started. It's what I was willing to do to live my dream, and there's not a day when I think it wasn't worth it.

What are you willing to do to make your bounce back everything you deserve it to be? I hope by now that the answer is, "Whatever it takes."

If you start off in a position that's not your dream spot, it doesn't mean that your bounce back is a failure or you are unqualified for bigger and better things. It does recognize the fact that we are living in shaky, uncertain times. There will be a good percentage of you who need to take a couple of steps backward in order to ultimately move forward. Don't be ashamed or afraid to do that—it's all part of the process. It might feel like a blow to your pride, but it ultimately will not be if you use the opportunity to impress the people around you.

With that in mind, I'm telling you it is perfectly okay to readjust your bounce back to fit the times in order to give you the best path to your ultimate goal.

Let me give you a great example from my current staff at Kentucky.

Many of you will remember Rod Strickland from his seventeen-year NBA career that saw him excel at the point guard spot for, among others, the New York Knicks and the Washington Wizards. I coached against Rod when I was with New Jersey, and he was one of those players you could never adequately prepare for—he was tough as nails and did all the little things to give his team the best chance at winning. He was quick, intuitive, and a magician with the ball. I've always felt he never got enough credit for his talents, but that happens in sports, and I've never heard Rod complain about such things.

A Bronx native who is legendary in New York City basketball circles, Rod had a standout career at DePaul University, where he led the program to four NCAA Tournament appearances and was a two-time All-American. He was drafted No. 18 overall in the 1988 NBA draft and sits among the Top 10 all-time assist leaders in the

NBA with 7,987 (a remarkable 7.3 assists per game). In the fall of 2008 he was inducted into the New York City Basketball Hall of Fame.

As you can see, Rod has a very impressive résumé, and his time in the NBA left him financially secure. He could have done anything he wanted and been his own boss for the rest of his life. But Rod had a different plan.

In mid-2006, word reached me that Rod, at forty years of age, was looking to get into college coaching, and I thought he'd be ideal for our program. His playing days were close enough that our players would be aware of who he was and of his accomplishments. I had success with ex-pros on my staff before, including Milt Wagner, who now coaches with Tony Barbee at UTEP.

When Rod and I talked for the first time, it was almost embarrassing to be offering the paltry package I had to a nearly twenty-year NBA veteran. But it was all I had.

"I'll do anything, Cal. Whatever you need," Rod told me, never once flinching over the money or the somewhat low stature of the job. He accepted a position as "director of student-athlete development/manager" that paid $1,200 a month for eight months—with *no* benefits and no guarantees of continued employment.

But Rod didn't care. "Just get me started," he kept saying. He wanted an opportunity to learn the coaching ropes and to pursue the next challenge in his storied career.

He did all the grunt work that first season with us. He checked to make sure players were going to classes and reported to me when they weren't. He spent hours and hours with our guys, retrieving balls and feeding passes.

"It was humbling," Rod said during the 2008–09 season. "There were awkward times, and I did wonder what I was thinking a few times. But that was part of the process and I accepted it."

I never once heard the word *no* from him. Nothing—I mean nothing—was beneath him. He'd just flash his million-dollar smile and go do whatever it was that needed doing.

Think about that. This was a guy who is right there alongside John Stockton, Magic Johnson, and Oscar Robertson on the career assists list, but he took an entry-level position to learn a new part of the trade. How many of us would accept a starting point so low after climbing so high? Not many, I guarantee you that.

I wasn't able to make his Hall of Fame induction in Manhattan, but so many of my friends called me to share just how emotional Rod got when he thanked me for "changing his life. Coach gave me direction and got me off the couch. My four children now see me working, and Cal has meant more to me, my wife, Cheryl, and my family than he'll ever know."

Thing is, I still look at it as Rod doing a favor for me and my program.

Hiring Rod has proven to be a godsend for both me and, as he will tell you, Rod. He was able to take classes at Memphis and worked toward completing his college degree (which he'll need if he wants to be a head coach), and he's an incredible resource for our players. They know about his career and respect what he has done. They go to him with all sorts of questions and concerns, and they have developed a great trust and bond with him. He was able to take young guys like Derrick Rose and Tyreke Evans under his wing and guide them through the rigors of being highly regarded freshmen. He has made himself indispensable to our program.

Rod told me he used to get so nervous before games that he would regularly throw up. So we talked to our kids about that, about dealing with nerves, fears, and anxieties. Rod let the guys know it's okay to have that feeling because he had it too. He has a lot to say about the importance of handling game pressure, and his words really register with the kids because they know that he's been there.

"I really like interacting with the kids. I bring a lot to the table, and, honestly, I've done it all," Rod said. "I know this game, and I know the life game too. I've made my mistakes, and I have a lot of info in this head. They know I'm going to give it to them straight."

Prior to our final season at Memphis, I was thrilled to be able to promote Rod to the position of director of basketball operations, which paid him in the six-figure range. When I took the Kentucky job, Rod came with me and I was able to promote him to a full-time assistant's spot. I know once he completes his degree (he's very close to doing so), he will undoubtedly have a future as a coach. If Rod wants to do the NBA thing as a coach, I think he'd have that opportunity. If there's an opportunity for him to be a head coach at the college level, he could do it. He's been through it all, and I know he'll be willing to do whatever it takes to reach his goal because I've seen him do that so many times already.

Rod's future has been cemented by his willingness to step back in order to move forward. He knew he'd need to take baby steps, and he didn't allow pride to get in the way of pursuing a new adventure. I can't tell you how much I admire that.

You see what I mean? Taking a position that is less glamorous than your last one isn't settling when you do it the right way. As long as you choose carefully and put yourself in a position where you are able to make incremental moves toward your ultimate goal, you will be serving yourself and your bounce back well. I'm not telling you to accept any first offer that comes your way. What I'm saying is that there are more important things than a title, especially when you get an opportunity to put yourself on a path to your long-term goals.

Let's not forget this point as you begin to examine your options closely. Be grateful and optimistic about the opportunity that lies in front of you. It may not feel perfect, but just getting back into play is crucial—get a foot in the door somewhere and then kick that door down.

> **PractiCal Point:** Acknowledge that taking a step backward to move forward is not the worst thing as long as you keep your ultimate goal in sight.

· · ·

Another component of what guys like Rod did was to allow themselves to be "reinvented" to a certain degree. For them, it meant staying in the sport they were most comfortable with and adjusting to different roles. In your case, it may mean going completely out of your comfort zone to another industry or to a different region of the country. Maybe it will entail finding a significant other who is nothing like the one you have been separated from.

You cannot be afraid to reinvent yourself. People do it *all* the time. Look at Al Gore. He was a few dangling chads away from being the most powerful man in the world, and when that fell through in unprecedented fashion, he reassessed where he was and where he wanted to be.

Rather than step back from public life to nurse his wounds, Al Gore started reinventing himself. He shifted his focus from governmental politics to the issues he cared most about. He dedicated his post-vice-presidential life to raising awareness about global warming and made one of the most important documentaries of the early twenty-first century, *An Inconvenient Truth*. All that did for him was help him win the 2007 Nobel Peace Prize! It's almost a certainty he wouldn't have made such an impact if he hadn't taken it upon himself to reinvent the way people perceived him.

Or how about this one: My good friend Mike Fratello became a full-time head coach in the NBA at the age of thirty-six with the Atlanta Hawks. He developed the Dominique Wilkins–led teams of the 1980s into one of the elite franchises, winning fifty or more games four seasons in a row. He was the NBA Coach of the Year for the 1985–86 season. In 1990, after seven seasons as head coach, Fratello was fired. The thinking at the time was that Mike would jump at the next open NBA job and resume his coaching career.

But Mike—who in addition to being a great friend is truly one of the best clinic and banquet speakers I have ever heard—was courted by television executives who loved his style and delivery. Instead of immediately getting back into the grind of coaching, Mike reinvented himself with NBC as an analyst alongside legendary play-by-play man Marv Albert. In no time, Marv and Mike developed a tremendous rapport and Mike was being hailed as a revelation in NBA broadcast circles. When Marv nicknamed him The Czar of the Telestrator for his unique ability to diagram and dissect plays, Mike's broadcasting career really took off. He eventually returned to coaching in 1993 with Cleveland (until 1999) and then in 2004 (through 2007) with the Memphis Grizzlies, where I got to know him even better. When he was fired in Cleveland, he again teamed with Marv; this time on TNT, and after the Grizzlies let him go, he went back to TNT (and also joined Marv on the YES network's New Jersey Nets package).

You have to give The Czar a lot of credit—he's been able to reinvent himself as a broadcaster but also maintain enough respect in the league to be rehired on two separate occasions. By remaining around the game and coaching seventeen seasons (with nearly seven hundred wins) Mike has extended his career and, in the process, found something he loves doing. It would not surprise me in the least to see Mike lead another NBA team to the playoffs.

You, too, can reinvent yourself at this point of your bounce back. You need to carefully contemplate what it will mean for you and think about what kinds of sacrifices you are and are not willing to make. But if you can dream it, I say you can do it.

"What I frequently ask people to do is think about something totally outside the box, something really different," career coach Bobbie LaPorte says. "I ask them to think about if they could do anything at all, if they didn't have to worry about money or responsibility. I'll even ask them to think about something they did as a kid they just loved. Or when they just felt so on top of the world, when they were 'in the zone' and everything was running on eight cylinders and they loved what they were doing."

I need you to realize that this bounce back you are going through can be a door opening, instead of one closing. Let me tell you what I tell my players when they're going through a little slump: I believe in you more than you believe in yourself.

Every one of my players is talented enough to do what we ask of him; if he weren't, he wouldn't be wearing a Kentucky uniform. The same holds true for you. You never would have reached this point in your bounce back if you weren't competent enough to be on my team. I don't settle for half effort or repeated mistakes—the definition of insanity is doing the same thing over and over again and expecting a different result.

Do not let that dysfunction be a part of your bounce back. If you weren't confident in your own abilities at this stage, you wouldn't be competent to move forward. **But you *are* competent, and because of that you should be confident.**

Now it is a question of honestly figuring out what you are looking for and prioritizing those needs. At that juncture, you will begin to not only develop your job targets, but you'll pick out specific targets to pursue as your bounce back reentry point.

> **PractiCal Point:** Gain a clear vision of what your reinvention might encompass and assess the reality of that visualization.

. . .

I don't have to tell you this, but I will anyway: make sure your targets are both specific and realistic. We'd all like to find a well-paying job with incredible perks set in a tropical paradise. But how likely is that? We'd all like to have Brad Pitt or Jessica Alba fall madly in love with us, but it's just not going to happen (no offense to you, of course!). I want you to always be aiming high, but that doesn't mean aiming for Fantasy Island.

You are at a point now where you have once again found your comfort zone and are thinking clearly but still being cautious and optimistic about everything you are doing. Perhaps you have been on a few dates with a potential companion, and you are now ready to bring things to the next level. (Hopefully you will have been a little more creative than I was in wooing Ellen. I used to think a movie was a great date. I've gotten better as time has gone by, although Ellen may not fully agree with that!)

Or maybe you are going to have to move out of a large house—a McMansion—that became too much of a cash drain; this is the juncture where you must pragmatically assess what your next home will be.

Other bounce backs could be vice-based, where those of you who may have been abusing alcohol or drugs or been living an unhealthy lifestyle are now taking real steps to gain back control of your life.

Bounce backs are as varied as the people who undergo them, but a common stage for everyone will be this vital portion, where you allow yourself to get into specifics about the position, role, or existence you are going to pursue. To put it in a business perspective and something that everyone can relate to, it's time to create your Mission Statement—what it is you are striving to become.

This can be a specific career-based statement such as, "Securing a sales-management role in a Fortune 500 company specializing in pharmaceuticals where I can coach, mentor, and lead staff."

Or it can be a softer statement and pertain to your personal life, such as, "Finding a significant other who will accept me for all that I am, someone I can share life's ups, downs, and in-betweens with. I want to have children, so the person must be open to starting a family."

What you are essentially doing with your personal mission statement is providing a baseline description of what it is you will be pursuing. You have already worked to develop the right attitude and the right image; now, you are creating a specific vision for what exactly it is that you want. From that well-thought-out and developed vision, you are positioning yourself to specifically and efficiently give your bounce back the best chance of success.

After you get comfortable with it—and you should not be afraid to let it percolate for a few days in addition to sharing it with your

Kitchen Cabinet and other trusted allies—I'd like you to then think of specific targets that wholly fit your mission statement. You might locate two or three companies that fit the description of where you want to be. Do some preliminary research into job availability and whether the company has offices in your preferred geographical locations. This is part of validating your targets and cannot be over-looked. The internet is a powerful tool for this type of research, but so are former colleagues and network connections you have developed. In the relationship scenario, maybe you have been dating or getting to know a few different people. Think honestly about whom you have connected with the best—and don't limit it to physical attraction or material wealth. You will most assuredly find yourself in the same (or worse) position you were in if you base any of your bounce-back decisions on superficial and frivolous desires.

Never underestimate the importance of research. Whether you're looking for a new job or a new home or even a new signifi-cant other, make sure that you investigate thoroughly. As uncouth as it may sound, this is an opportune time to google the person, house/neighborhood, company, etc. you may be pursuing. Don't feel sneaky or untrusting when you do such background checking; it's just a safety mechanism to ensure you're not going too far down the road with the wrong choice. And you won't be the only one doing it either; someone will probably be checking you out online to see what sort of information is available on you out there. If it makes you feel better, you should also google yourself every so often to confirm there are no negative or damning mistruths being perpetuated on the World Wide Web.

That was something I faced a bit in 2000 when I began to ear-nestly pursue my next college-coaching position. Back when I was negotiating the final details of my contract with the New Jersey Nets, a story broke in the *Hartford Courant* alleging my star player at UMass, Marcus Camby—the 1996 National Player of the Year—had accepted cash and jewelry from two prospective agents while he was playing for the Minutemen. The timing was awkward to say the least, and when news of my accepting the Nets job surfaced, people immediately assumed I was leaving UMass to get away from the NCAA investigation that would follow the *Courant's* allegations.

Nothing could have been further from the truth—I had been talking to the Nets well before the Camby story came out. In fact, when the news of Marcus's alleged improprieties surfaced, I was strongly considering staying at UMass to fight the allegations and clear the university and myself from any wrongdoing. But in this case, perception was reality, and the media made it a point to suggest I was fleeing a sinking ship. Not until I was comfortable that the university and my staff had done everything the right way during Marcus's time at UMass did I accept the job in New Jersey.

While the "Camby situation," as it became known, would not affect my professional coaching career, it was still a concern that one day it might hinder future college prospects. The NCAA wound up vacating UMass's Final Four appearance, and the university was ordered to repay its $150,000 share of tournament proceeds. I felt awful about all of that, but it was important for me to let people know the NCAA concluded I was nothing more than a bystander in a bad position.

Marcus is one of the best people I've ever coached. He admitted he took $1,800 from what is known as a "runner"—someone who works on an agent's behalf to try and steer potential pros to that specific agent for purposes of representation—between his sophomore and junior years while he was at home in Hartford during the summer. He was taken advantage of by greedy, unscrupulous people, and he paid the price—literally. Not only did he agree to talk to the NCAA to explain what had happened (a rarity in NCAA investigations), but he repaid UMass the $150,000 it lost from the vacating of the Final Four appearance.

At the end of the day, if anyone looked into the violation or checked with the NCAA, they would be told unequivocally that my actions were ethical and UMass had done everything in its power to prevent such wrongdoings. Marcus made a poor decision and succumbed to temptation. He admitted the error of his ways and took a hit to his reputation. (I'm happy to say Marcus bounced back and is in the midst of a successful decade-plus NBA career.) Still, if anyone googled my name and Marcus's, they would inevitably come across false accusations and innuendo. Because of all that, I still keep a copy of the June 8, 2004, letter the NCAA sent me exonerating me from any involvement in Marcus's cautionary tale. It came from Tom Yeager, the then-chairman of the NCAA committee on infractions, and said in part, "The committee fully recognizes you had nothing to with the violations of Marcus Camby during the 1995–96 season. In a sense, you were an innocent victim."

At the time I was looking for a job in 2000, I was very aware that potential employers would have questions on the Camby situation, and I was well prepared to answer those questions and defend my record and actions. If there are questionable behaviors or ambiguous information floating in the webosphere about you, be prepared to answer whatever questions may arise from potential partners, employers, or friends. It's like lawyers—they never want to be blindsided in court by details their client had neglected to mention. You don't want there to be any confusion or uncertainty about your public record, especially when you are interviewing for a job.

With all your ducks in a row and your mind focused on securing the best possible bounce-back reentry point, you are now prepared to zero in on your target. Nothing impresses potential employers more than having an interviewee come in with a thorough understanding of the business and job he or she is interested in.

"If you have done your homework, you can honestly state that you have studied all that is publicly available about Company X," career coach Bobbie LaPorte told me.

Also, according to Bobbie, this is a time when you can tap into industry websites and professional associations where there may even be career guidance tips and other helpful resources.

For that type of research, Bobbie suggested job aggregator sites like www.indeed.com to get a feel for typical job requirements, salary ranges, and which companies are more likely to be hiring. Other career networking sites such as www.LinkedIn.com and www.plaxo.com are great for locating former coworkers and friends who can connect you with people and companies that may be looking for help. Sites like www.imantri.com offer a peer-to-peer community where you can find mentors and coaches to aid in your search.

"I'd also encourage people to take informational interviews with people currently doing the jobs they might be interested in, if they haven't done so already," Bobbie said. "There are all sorts of industry conferences, job clinics, and networking gatherings to attend as well."

When it's all said and done, though, it's the work you do on your own that will ultimately give you the best insight into what your approach should be. Hearing and discussing are both valuable tools, but the true test will be what your gut and your mind are telling you.

> **PractiCal Point:** Focus on a concrete mission objective that will serve as your bounce-back reentry point, and maintain the same vigorous and unyielding attitude you've established throughout these weeks, months, and years.

CHAPTER 10

CHOOSE WISELY

TARGET YOUR REENTRY OPPORTUNITY,
AND PURSUE IT DILIGENTLY

I can't claim my reentry job search took a traditional path, but I do know many of the steps we undertook to wind up at Memphis in 2000 will mimic the phases at this stage of your bounce back. I did my best to leave no stone unturned the further along I got in the process, and I urge you to be just as meticulous.

Right now, your goal should be to bounce back, not bounce around. By this I mean that you have to wait for the right opportunity and understand that in some cases, the next job you take may be necessary to set you up for the real job you want *after* that one. If you feel like a position is a good stepping-stone, go for it. Trust in yourself, in your own judgment and your own expertise. There's no shame in accepting a job that will give you leverage for an even better one.

I actually experienced as much when I was at Kansas. I'm not sure how many people know this story. I had served one season (1982–83) as a volunteer assistant under longtime KU head coach Ted Owens, who was fired in 1983 after two sub-.500 seasons (despite 341 wins

over nearly twenty seasons). I knew it was time for me to start searching for another job.

What I found was a job in the Northeast with University of Ver-
mont coach Bill Whitmore, who hired me as the Catamounts' recruiting coordinator. I was on campus in Burlington a few weeks—just
long enough to have a head shot taken for the media guide—when
I received a call from Coach Brown, who had been hired to replace
Ted. He offered me a spot on his staff as what they called at the time
a "part-time assistant," but it was a full-time job. I logically looked
at the situation and put all emotions aside, which is something very
important to keep in mind during your bounce back. UVM was a
good opportunity for me, and I know I could have done well there.
But Kansas was a *great* opportunity. I felt awful and apologized pro-
fusely about leaving Coach Whitmore in the lurch, but it was something I had to do, and he understood it—things like that happen all
the time, especially in the coaching profession.

If the person who hired you really cares about you, he or she will
not begrudge you for taking an opportunity with more potential. If
that person flips out and vows revenge on you, he or she didn't care
about you in the first place, and you have to realize it wouldn't have
been a good situation in the long run. I always stayed in touch with
Coach Whitmore, and he has been to a game or two of ours in the
intervening years. I still sometimes think of how different things
might have been if I stayed at UVM—there may never have been the
incredible Tom Brennan–era (he replaced Coach Whitmore in 1986)
had I stayed! I'm joking Tom! Coach Brennan did an unbelievable
job at UVM, and I will always remember watching his team upset
Syracuse in the 2005 NCAA Tournament.

I kept my heart out of the decision and assessed Coach Brown's offer from the business and career-development side. I researched my options and knew all about the pluses and minuses of both jobs.

I'll tell you another story from when I had to make this same kind of decision during my bounce back. I began to seriously target college jobs that interested me while in my sixth month with Larry Brown in Philadelphia. It's usually mid to late February when the media starts to heavily speculate on which college coaches are on the "hot seat" and who will be moving from one job to another. (Though even that is changing now as more and more coaches are getting pushed out or being let go in January, the way Mark Gottfried [Alabama] and Dennis Felton [Georgia] were during the 2008–09 season. These days it seems like change happens more frequently and more unpredictably than ever.)

In truth, those winter months can be one of the worst times of the year for many coaches—whether they're facing the prospect of losing a job or are in a position to take a better one. It's such a crucial time of the season—fighting for league titles, NCAA Tournament bids, and seeding—and outside distractions tend to make it even harder to prepare your team for the stretch run.

We were having a pretty good year with the 76ers (eventually finishing 49–43 and advancing to the Eastern Conference semifinals), and Coach was supportive of whatever I had to do.

Around the middle of December, a few intermediaries began to contact me to gauge my interest in a few of those college jobs that were likely to be opening in March. One thing led to another, and eventually the Memphis athletic director R.C. Johnson and I had a brief phone conversation where we mostly introduced ourselves to each other. That call was based more on our common experiences from the Atlantic 10 when I was at UMass, and R.C. was the AD at

Temple—we had some real battles with the Owls and their legendary coach John Chaney. R.C. and Bob Marcum, my former boss at UMass, were pretty friendly, so we immediately had a connection through Bob as well. (You see how prior relationships can always help you down the road? Keep that in mind as you continue your search, and don't be afraid to reach out even to those people you may have lost touch with.)

From that phone call, we eventually decided it would be good to meet face-to-face. In the latter half of December, we had our first of several "secret meetings," this one in Chicago. That initial meeting was probably the most important one—for both of us. We had dinner together and a long conversation and really started to get to know each other. We hit it off pretty well and spent some more time together the next morning.

We vowed to stay in touch with each other. No promises were made, but there was interest from both sides. My curiosity had been stimulated enough to start doing some due diligence on the University of Memphis and the city itself.

I knew very little about the Memphis program. I remembered the 1980s when they were a perennial NCAA Tournament team out of the old Metro Conference.

I knew much less about the city of Memphis. Other than knowing it was the place where Dr. Martin Luther King Jr. was tragically gunned down at the Lorraine Motel, the location of Elvis Presley's Graceland Mansion, and the home to great barbecue ribs, I was very underinformed about the Bluff City.

I would have been cheating myself if I didn't do the most I could to replace my ignorance with knowledge. I'll be perfectly honest though; when I was first contacted about the Memphis job, my initial thought was, *It's not exactly what I'm looking for.*

Thankfully, I didn't let that first impression impede my research, and neither should you in your own bounce back. The more I learned, the more appealing the job became, and I realized it was just the chance I'd been waiting for.

> **PractiCal Point:** Research whatever the opportunity is that is in your sights, and then research and investigate some more *and* be sure to keep emotions out of your decisions and pursuits.

• • •

As I did with all the possibilities I was hearing about, I bounced the Memphis job off Coach Brown. He was a key member of my Kitchen Cabinet then, as he is now, and there was just about no one better in basketball to discuss college programs with than he. He had deep and personal history with two of the most revered programs in the nation—Kansas and UCLA—and his connections throughout all of basketball meant more information was only a phone call away.

"I interviewed for the head coach's job at Memphis in 1979 when they were still Memphis State," Coach Brown told me when I first brought up the job. "I wound up removing my name and went to UCLA for two years. But I remember a lot of good things about that situation there."

"I loved that job then, John, and I love it now. Especially for you," Coach Brown said. "You can really build that thing. It's similar to UMass in a lot of ways, and look what you did there."

In addition to tapping into Coach Brown's knowledge base, I started to reach out to friends in the coaching fraternity and athletic directors who were familiar with the Memphis program. Specifically, I began to talk—in confidence—to a few other coaches in the Tigers' league, Conference USA, whom I was close with and whom I knew I could trust. Through Bob Marcum, I was able to get a feel for other athletic directors' impressions of the school.

"Basketball is king in that city, John," Bob said. "It's one heck of a job, it really is. Of all the jobs available, it may be the one that fits you best."

When I asked Bruiser Flint what he thought of the job, he, too, raved about the city always producing great players. "They've got great tradition, Cal, and you could get it done there. It's a good situation for you; the only thing I'm not sure about is how you'll adjust to the Mid-South. It's different down there from up here in the Northeast," he told me.

I filed away all the opinions I was receiving at the time and valued the input from my Kitchen Cabinet and others.

Likewise, you need to reach out to those who have prior knowledge of the position, person, home, or whatever it is you are pursuing. You need to emphasize you're keeping things on the down low and would appreciate their discretion in not sharing your interest with anyone else. Sometimes you create unnecessary competition for yourself when you begin to poke around the edges of your pursuit. Others will start saying, "Hmmmm, what does *he* see in that job that I don't?" That happens all the time in college basketball and in the business world.

I continued to do my research, but at the same time, I started making a list of the concerns I had about what the Memphis job would entail and if it was really the best spot for me to have my bounce back. This is a very natural thing for anyone going through a change, and the most important thing is to be aware of what your concerns are so that you can go about getting answers. But the thing I was able to do—and what you need to do—was listen more to the positives than focusing on the negatives. I tried to find balance between the two, which you need to be doing at all times. But you also have to be honest about your uncertainties so you can either refute or confirm those fears.

There were issues—conference affiliation, a change of the school's president, and declining attendance, among others—and uncertainties I needed to have addressed before I could seriously think about being the head coach at Memphis. It very well could have been a hornet's nest.

As I set about my research, it became apparent that the obstacles I foresaw were not as dire as they may have at first seemed. In fact, a lot were similar to struggles we faced in the early days at UMass. Realizing that brought me some relief, because I knew we had overcome complications of that nature before.

This is a time when you can tap into your prior life experiences and understand that every new opportunity comes with inherent hurdles. Remember, you were able to clear those hindrances before and you will surely be able to do it again—this time armed with the knowledge that your instincts and approaches are proven.

Every job, relationship, and circumstance is hard. In my profession, we are sometimes beholden to things well beyond our control.

Every college coach out there has a hard job. You can never please everybody. If you listen to people in the seats, soon enough you're going to be sitting with them. But what I realized was that I was up for the challenges that Memphis would pose—in fact, I was excited about them. You've got to block out the naysayers and be strong-willed and realize you're doing everything for substantial reasons—to help the program around you grow and to have an impact on the young men's lives. Do not look at these perceived problems as setbacks, but instead view them as your latest prospects.

I'm not going to tell you all my fears were alleviated through my research and, in fact, I was still bothered a bit that there wasn't huge interest in the Memphis job. Did other people know things I didn't? This is a common fear and certainly one worth considering— but just because a new opportunity may not be right for someone else, it could still be a Godsend for you. My mind was eased even more when I learned that Athletic Director R.C. Johnson was keeping things close to the vest because he had Johnny Jones, his interim coach, still in place.

To his credit, Johnny did a fantastic job of keeping the team together amid the turmoil and even got on a little winning streak heading into the conference tournament in 2000. There was a vocal section of people in town who wanted Johnny (who is African American) to be given the full-time position. If he somehow got the Tigers to the NCAA Tournament by winning the Conference USA Tournament, it would have been close to impossible for R.C. to hire a replacement.

But R.C. and I stayed in constant contact and I had a few separate meetings with him and also the school's outgoing president Dr. V. Lane Rawlins.

The oft-told (by me!) story about how we agreed to my salary on a cocktail napkin is true. It's also true that I was very interested in tying in our academic success to reasonable bonuses for myself and my staff. I wanted to show how we were committed to not just turning out players but to helping young men get their educations and better themselves—the same way we had at UMass.

"If we graduate 60 percent of our players and win 70 percent of our games, I want a bonus of $100,000," I told R.C. and Lane.

"Fine," they both said quickly.

I figured they were so agreeable to that, I might as well push it a bit.

"And, if we hit that graduation rate and win 80 percent of our games, it's a $200,000 bonus."

Again, neither flinched. "Fine," R.C. said.

Boy, that was easy, I thought. It wasn't until a few weeks later that I discovered why they may have been so amenable to those two incentive clauses: The University of Memphis had not graduated a scholarship freshman from 1989–1996, according to university records. In fact, from December 1991 through August 2000, just six scholarship men's basketball players graduated. I never imagined the number could be so low.

Let my mistake be a valuable lesson for you in the art of negotiating and researching: always know what it is you're negotiating for. I knew there was a low graduation rate, but I hadn't gotten the hard, cold numbers. If I had, I might have started out with different numbers.

(I am most proud to say that when I left Memphis in 2009, we had graduated nineteen of twenty-three players since the 2002–03 season and from December 2000 through May 2009 twenty-five scholarship men's basketball players graduated.)

In late February, R.C. and his staff "snuck" me into Memphis so I could get a look around. The Memphis team was away for a game at Marquette, so I was better able to visit under the radar.

About midway through my visit, I began to really believe Memphis was a sleeping giant. I was blown away by the city, and I was floored by all I was seeing around me. They had some great basketball history.

I was quickly convinced that if the community truly wanted a national program, they could have one. In the course of about thirty-six hours, I went from questioning whether I wanted the job to the anxiety of thinking, *I've got to have this job*. I knew I could awaken the sleeping giant. Memphis had the foundation in place to compete year in and year out with college basketball's elite.

While I was strongly leaning toward agreeing to the job if it was indeed offered, the path was not entirely cleared.

> **PractiCal Point:** Do your homework and be prepared to capitalize on the best available opportunity.

• • •

Before my reentry opportunity could fully crystallize, there were still issues that needed resolving. Mainly, I began to experience the natural and expected condition of "apprehension invention." You know what I'm talking about. It can strike at any time. Maybe you're in the department store, and you're deciding between two coats. You finally settle on one, and just as you're heading to the register, you turn around and look back at the rack where you left choice number two. For a moment, maybe more, you're thinking about all the things the other coat has to offer that your choice doesn't—a heavier lining, the inside pocket for your cell phone, a more versatile color—whatever it is.

What you're doing at that moment is inventing reasons to be apprehensive. I'm certainly not comparing your bounce-back reentry to the buying of a coat, but something in our makeup always seems to bring us to the "what if" when making significant decisions. Instead, we should be saying, "go for it."

At that time, I said to myself, *Maybe I'm just not meant to get this job. If that's the case, Lord, I'm fine with it.* It's the same thing I would say eight years later as I watched our lead evaporate against Kansas in the title game.

Whether you're a religious person or more of a spiritual one, I think there are certain times in life when you have to look at a situation and say to yourself, *If it's meant to be, it will be.* If it's not, there must be a grander vision for what will happen to you. Always keep that in mind, especially if you don't get the first job you go after or lose out on the first house you make an offer on. You need to believe, as I do, that all things come in due time.

Your next move may not be entirely on your terms, but you have to be willing to risk it all and turn the situation into what you want it to be. **Part of writing your own story means you must also pursue the ending you envisioned.**

You have to be sure you are comfortable with the move you're making and committed to putting your heart and soul into the situation. This is also the time when you can reflect on what you've done to get to this point of your bounce back and take pride in the path you have followed. You must be prepared for the hard work that still lies ahead. In some senses, your bounce back is just the beginning of the rest of your life.

PractiCal Point: Be at peace with your decision, and know you are about to embark on an unimaginable journey of joy.

• • •

I want to step away from my reentry opportunity with Memphis for a few moments and share with you a bit of the process I went through in late March 2009 when Kentucky contacted me about their vacant head-coaching position. As you read over the following paragraphs, I want you to compare my approach in contemplating the Kentucky job versus that of the Memphis job.

My Kentucky hiring process began shortly after we were eliminated from the 2009 NCAA Tournament by Missouri on March 26 in Phoenix, Arizona. We had won twenty-seven games in a row leading up to that game, but we ran into a very hot and very well-coached team led by Mike Anderson. I was so incredibly proud of our Memphis team because they played the entire year with the weight of expectations on them as fans and media tried to measure them at every turn against our Final Four team of the year before. It is the price of success that expectations sometimes get out of whack, and athletes and coaches accept that as part of the deal.

As they had all year, the team fought to the very end and despite losing by eleven points, there were still glimmers of hope all the way into the final minute of the game. I remember sitting in my hotel room after the game with a few assistants and close friends and being completely drained. I wasn't happy with the loss, but I did take comfort in knowing I would be able to spend some quiet time with Ellen and the kids while I unwound and decompressed.

I had no idea that things were about to get ramped up instead.

By the time we returned to Memphis on that Friday, word had spread through college basketball that Kentucky head coach Billy Gillispie—on the job just two years—had been fired. There had been rumors for days, but when it was made official I started to think back two years prior, when the job was open and I wondered to myself whether Kentucky officials would call to test my interest.

The call never came. It was a blessing that it didn't because I was able to coach two more incredibly rewarding and meaningful seasons at Memphis. We made our title game run in 2007–08 while winning an NCAA record 38 games and followed it up with our 33-win, Sweet 16 season. All four seniors on the 2008–09 season graduated in four years and six of the players were given opportunities to play professional basketball in the U.S. It was an amazing ride for so many reasons, so looking back I was glad no offer was made in 2007.

All things for a reason, you have to remember.

But with the Kentucky job open again, the call did come and I had to listen. A few intermediaries from Kentucky called to gauge my interest. It wasn't that I was looking to get out of Memphis. Quite the opposite, really. I was comfortable in Memphis and so was my family. We were entrenched in the community and had grown to love the area. The program had a bright future and it appeared as though we would be able to continue to make strides, although I knew it would be close to impossible to feed the beast we had created.

When you do find yourself in this situation, and I know you will, you need to look around and ask yourself, "Have I done all I can at this particular place?" If the answer is yes, you need to seriously consider the possibilities of the new situation.

The question was difficult for me to answer, and it was made even more taxing because the interest was coming from KENTUCKY! Kentucky basketball: *the* most storied program in history and one that had fallen on some hard times (at least by its own lofty standards; they hang banners for one reason and one reason alone in Lexington, and that is for national titles). It is, in my opinion, the apex of coaching in all of sports. Period.

Recruiting had fallen off, the fan base was getting restless, and the "brand" needed to be rebuilt and reestablished. I knew all of that.

What I didn't know was how committed the school's president, Dr. Lee Todd, and the school's athletic director, Mitch Barnhart, were to bringing the glory back to Lexington.

As conversations continued, it became apparent to me that I could make a difference at Kentucky. I've told many colleagues over the years, "If you think you make a difference and have an impact, you should go for it."

When I was able to sit down with Dr. Todd, Mitch, and other key members of the university, the question I needed to have answered was not about winning but about how we would treat our student athletes. What I needed to know is that I wouldn't be working for people who would throw student-athletes under the bus at the first sign of a misstep. I have coached a long time, and like my own children, players will do dumb, immature things. Few of us can honestly say we didn't do some of the very same things. When they do make poor decisions, it is our job to get them to take responsibility and change. As educators, we must allow them that opportunity.

When I was comfortable that we were on the same page with that issue, it became apparent that my other desires were very much in line with Dr. Todd's vision for the university. When I talked about the brand slipping and my ideas for bringing it back to its rightful perch in college basketball, I could sense their commitment would be complete and unyielding. We all wanted to do things with strict adherence to NCAA guidelines and we all wanted to bring the program back to the community—back to the Big Blue Nation that is like no other group of fans in the country.

While all those factors made it easy to see the upside of the Kentucky job, I struggled mightily with leaving Memphis after putting all those years of sweat and hard work into the program. I was proud of the program we had built.

I'm giving you the inside story on my experience so you will understand everything you are doing is going to lead to amazing opportunities. Your dreams can come true.

I never—not in a million years—thought I would be putting the finishing touches on this book from behind my desk in the Joe Craft Center at the University of Kentucky. But I am and I am humbled and honored to be the head coach of the Wildcats.

What was it my mother always told me? "If you can dream it, Johnny, you can be it."

That goes for all of us.

> **PractiCal Point:** All the energy you are putting into your bounce back now will serve you many years down the road and position you for the very best that life has to offer.

. . .

PRACTICE PLAN # 5
CONTROL
THE INTERVIEW

EMPHASIS OF THE DAY: Take command of your interview through preparation and scripting.

You are at the point of your bounce back where it will soon be time to have a key interview or important meeting. This drill prepares you to be the master of that discussion, and by doing so, you will be in the position to choose your reentry opportunity and not have it chosen for you.

PURPOSE

For several years now—going all the way back to when I first met with the UMass search committee in 1988—I have kept a list with pointers to use when interviewing, negotiating, and discussing business opportunities. I hold this list very close to me, and the only people I share it with are coaches on my "tree" who are preparing for job interviews and a select number of our extended "family" members. Everyone from John Robic (Youngstown State) to Bruiser Flint (UMass and Drexel) to Tony Barbee (UTEP) to the most recent head coaches on my tree (Derek Kellogg at UMass and Chuck Martin at Marist) have been privy to the information and guidance on the sheet. It's become a sort of holy grail for the Calipari coaching tree. Bru takes great pride in having been the first one to use it for an interview he had at Northeastern University in Boston.

"It went okay, but the athletic director I interviewed with, Barry Gallup, called Cal afterward and told him some of the things I didn't do so well with," Bru said. "It was my first time, I was nervous, and it was a great opportunity for me to see how the process went. I'm still grateful for that chance."

From then on, however, I said, "That won't happen again with one of my guys. We will all be prepared, and we will help one another to prepare."

"The main thing is to control the conversation," Bru said. "And no one controls the conversation like the guy who came up with the guidelines!"

Since you are on my team, you're entitled to a partial look at what the five-page document contains. Its message is really quite simple: control the interview, hit on your key strengths, and present a confident leader whom any executive or superior would kill for to have on his or her team.

DRILL

In this drill, I want you to get a feel for how important it is to be overprepared and poised when your time comes to meet with decision makers who will affect your bounce back—whatever you are coming back from.

Just as a quick frame of reference, prior to Derek Kellogg's job interview at UMass in the spring of 2008, we went over the guiding principles several times in my office and over meals. When we thought Derek was ready, John Robic and I rehearsed with him over a series of four walks around the Memphis campus. We would ask Derek the types of questions the search committee might ask him, and he was required to answer back the way he would in the interview.

Let me tell you, on that first walk, John and I were looking at each other and trying to contain our laughter over Derek's fumbling and bumbling. But by the third walk he was on point and polished, so much so that several of my old UMass connections called after his interview to tell me how much Derek impressed everybody with his composure and vision. "It put him over the top, no question," one friend said.

WATCH ME FIRST

The first thing the Calipari Interviewing Guidelines emphasize—and maybe the most vital—is for you to set the tone early in your interview. I've found the best way to do this is to have five strategic points you will focus on. For coaching candidates, I recommend Discipline, Structure, Academics, Recruiting Philosophy, and Style of Play. When appropriate, you need to be able to spell out a two-, three-, four-year, and beyond plan for each of those categories; interviewers want to see that you have foresight for your long- and short-term goals and realistic expectations for how you can accomplish them.

What follows is a rather extreme example, exaggerated for emphasis, but it helps demonstrate the approach:

Most of the time, an AD or a member of the search committee will pick up the interview candidate at the airport. Small talk inevitably ensues.

"How was your flight?" the school's representative might ask.

"Great. Everything was fine; I really appreciate this opportunity," my guy will say. "You know what else I appreciate? How kids all want structure in their lives. That's exactly what I want to instill in the program—structure, responsibility, and the ability to have our young men bring out their best every day."

That's an extreme example of a hard sell that is not actually necessary, but you get the idea. You don't want to come off as overly aggressive or arrogant, but you want to gain control of the process from the get-go and be sure you get to address those five key points you have determined will be the focus of your interview.

Beyond the basics of good interviewing techniques—sit up straight, be engaging, etc.—it's always a good idea to have some key buzz words and terms interspersed throughout your interview, words that will stick in the minds of people you are meeting with. For coaching positions, some of the ones I encourage would be "academic achievement," "community involvement," "positively representing the university," "and winning in the classroom and on the court."

It's also mandatory that you know your own greatest assets and continually sprinkle words and terms like "versatility," "commitment," "team player," "diverse background," "efficient," "ambitious," and "enthusiastic" throughout your dialogue with potential employers.

These tips may seem rudimentary, but they are worth emphasizing, and you can't argue with our coaching family's success rate, either, as this approach has helped no fewer than six of my former assistants land head jobs—usually on their first attempt at gaining a position.

I still remember what then–Memphis President Lane Rawlins told the local paper upon my hiring: "There are questions I like to ask about [academics]. He addressed them without my having to even ask."

One last point to stress from my guidelines is probably the simplest of all: when you're done presenting all your points, stop talking.

It's like that in recruiting too. Say your piece and be done, because the next word you say could be the wrong one!

I now want you to make a list of your five strategic points, and take time to refine and get comfortable with your central themes. Remember to be as specific as possible, but also succinct and direct.

SECTION III

. . .

YOU
MADE
IT

CHAPTER 11

NEW BEGINNINGS

YOUR SECOND LIFE
CAN BE BETTER THAN YOUR FIRST

S ince you joined my team, there hasn't been much time to sit back and soak in all that you have accomplished. We've been going at a hectic pace, and that has been intentional—the busier you are, the less time you will have to reflect or rue. Now, however, for at least a few moments, you need to take a deep breath and pat yourself on the back. After all, what are accomplishments worth if you don't take time to enjoy and appreciate them?

This chapter commences the final phase of your bounce back, and for this and the next three chapters, we will put you in a position to make the most of whatever your opportunity may be—whether it's a career opportunity, a new significant other, a new home, or any type of fresh start. As you will learn, your bounce back never ends—never—but how you handle the early point will go a long way in defining just how close your bounce back will be to the story you wrote after chapter 6.

You have now worked to the point where you have secured your reentry opportunity and this rebirth. This is no small achievement, and your success gives me great pride, knowing that you are a valued bounce-back team member.

You have your swagger back, and now we need to make sure that swagger doesn't turn to arrogance. Your journey is far from over, so don't give in to the urge to sit back and admire your work. As hard as you worked to get here, you will now need to work that much harder to cultivate and sustain the success you know you deserve.

Don't kid yourself—there will be more detours along the way. Pitfalls and U-turns are all part of the reentry opportunity you have created for yourself. Everything we have done to this point to condition you will allow you to face those challenges and conquer them.

You know the value of staying in the moment, and that insight will serve you well. **Don't allow your dreams to become daydreams.** You need to have a plan of attack, work day to day, and show consistent effort. When I have a player who is struggling shooting the ball, the first thing my staff and I will ask of the young man is to get in the gym and get extra shots up. I need to see the player putting in extra effort to overcome his struggles—and not just for a week or two weeks, but every day so that he will see change from week to week and month to month. Nothing happens overnight on the basketball court or in life. Once you begin to string days of improvement together and see the extra work paying off, you will find yourself craving that additional time, knowing it is making you better.

What I'm going to ask of you, now that you have your reentry opportunity, is to put in an extra hour of work every day. Sixty minutes, that's all. You see, those extra minutes are going to be what separates you from everyone else. When your coworker is leaving at 6 p.m. feeling satisfied that he or she worked extra time, you are going to keep at it until 7 p.m. Don't just sit there and think, *Well, I'm here and no one else is*; instead, make productive use of that time, and revel in the knowledge that soon 1 hour will become 5, 5 will become 20, and 20 will become 240 over the course of year. Think of how far ahead you will be with what amounts to *six* extra forty-hour weeks of effort per year.

> **PractiCal Point:** Take pride in where you have landed in your bounce back, but also realize the hard work is far from over.

• • •

In chapter 7, we discussed the conference-play portion of your bounce back. We said it would last a few weeks or months and it would be vital in preparing you for the final, distinct phase. Once you have taken a new position, found a new significant other, and have begun to live your "second life," you are prepared for the "post-season," the equivalent of what my team goes through from mid-March into, hopefully, early April when the Final Four is held. For us, it consists of our Conference Tournament, the announcement of the NCAA Tournament field (Selection Sunday, as it's become known), and then the actual "Big Dance" itself.

Let me just go back to one thing before we get into making the most of your bounce back. I want to examine the term "second life." I picked up on this view from an extraordinary man whose story I learned about through some friends in the University of Massachusetts community. The story of Glenn Mangurian's incredible bounce back captures the meaning of "second life" better than anything I could ever hope to write, so here it is:

Glenn earned his undergraduate degree in mathematics (1970) and his MBA (1973) from UMass. He was and is what the alums like to call a "true Umie." Glenn left Amherst and built a wonderful life for himself, his wife, and their two children, eventually settling in a tony community on the south shore of Boston. He rose to the level of senior vice president of CSC Index, an international consultancy firm based in Cambridge, Massachusetts, where Glenn helped to commercialize the concept of Business Reengineering—a concept of workflow efficiency that gained popularity in the mid-1990s. After an acquisition of the company, Glenn was a member of the leadership team that reinvented the firm and grew annual revenues from $25 million to $200 million. He established himself as an innovator and a corporate leader who is well respected and admired in his field. Glenn is a true success story and a testament to what hard work and treating people the right way will give rise to. In 1999 he founded his own consultancy firm, Frontier Works (www.frontierworks.com), focusing on market-growth opportunities for individuals and businesses.

His path had led him to a more-than-comfortable life filled with family, friends, and travel. He was doing what he loved and helping others in the process.

Then, on May 26, 2001, Glenn, who was fifty-two at the time, was preparing for his daughter Laura's high school graduation party to be held in the family's backyard. He was working outside with his wife, Gail, sprucing up the yard for the party when he felt some lingering back pain for which he had taken some Advil earlier in the day. He left the yard, went into his house, and "whatever happened, happened. It felt like I was being stabbed in the back."

He wound up on the floor of his kitchen in excruciating pain, thinking that lying down would help the pain subside.

"It didn't," he said. "My son Mark [twelve at the time] and my wife were home, and I told Gail she needed to call the EMTs."

In those moments, his life changed forever. He was rushed to a local hospital south of Boston and eventually to the Boston Medical Center. Doctors determined Glenn had suffered an unprovoked disc rupture that pressed against his spinal cord. They informed him the lower half of his body was permanently paralyzed.

In mere hours, Glenn went from preparing for one of the happiest days of his life—his daughter's high school graduation—to dealing with an unthinkable tragedy that would forever alter his existence.

He went through two lengthy operations and spent two months in the New England Regional Spinal Cord Injury Center and another four years in physical therapy.

"I was healthy and secure in my career as a management consultant, and in an instant, my life was utterly transformed and filled with uncertainty," Glenn wrote in a phenomenally motivational *Harvard Business Review* article from March 2007, titled "Realizing What You Are Made Of." "At first, I was mostly frightened and in serious pain. Then I felt anger and sadness at losing the use of my legs . . .

"I've had some very dark days and life is a constant struggle," he wrote. "But at the same time the experience has allowed me to take stock of all that I have, rediscover some of the neglected parts of my life, and cut through the clutter to focus on what is really consequential."

Glenn is incredibly resilient, and intelligent enough to understand his situation was what it was. "I couldn't change the past," he said.

I asked Glenn how soon after his trigger event he was able to gain that type of perspective?

"After the operations, when I woke up and had some time to think over what had occurred, I started processing what had happened," Glenn said when we talked to him over the course of writing this book. "Very quickly I was struck by the notion that my first life was over.

"I reconciled that it had been a good life," he said. "Prior to injury my nature was to never second-guess things from my past; I would never look back. Thankfully that skill/habit carried forward."

Admittedly, the reality of what Glenn was going through was a shock to his whole family and his entire network of friends and associates.

"As time went on, and the days turned into weeks, I started getting scores of notes from people I had known throughout my life, telling me about specific instances of when and how I helped them through rough spots in their lives," Glenn said. "It was almost like an [unending] eulogy, and that was an odd sensation. But those notes and cards reinforced that my first life wasn't *just* good, it was great.

"To know I had made a difference in peoples' lives was a liberating experience," Glenn said. "I then went through a period of time celebrating my first life and not so much mourning it. I retained that skill of being able to look inward and reflect on things, but not rue or regret."

In fact, Glenn said, a lot of the things he did in that first life seem unreal to him now. He sometimes recalls and wonders if he really did all the things he managed to accomplish in his first fifty-plus years.

"I would travel all over for work," he said. "You know the deal—up early to catch the 6 a.m. flight to somewhere and then making it home to coach my daughter's softball or be home for the family. I had to pinch myself sometimes to make sure those memories were real."

In his second life, Glenn took to reconnecting with old friends and associates he had long ago lost contact with. That process—mostly through the internet—helped him transition more into his new way of living.

"The further away I got from my point of injury, I also began to look at my first life and saw some holes in it. I wanted to make sure my 'second life' filled in some of the gaps. There was something there where I needed to have a connection to all parts of my first life and especially people I had lost contact with. It was an important step for me to take. It helped in celebrating many aspects of my 'first life.'"

Glenn's words and his story can serve as inspiration for us all. One of the things that resonated most with me when reading about and hearing Glenn's explanation of his "two lives" is what he made sure to do with his second opportunity.

"My 'first life' was much more programmed, but that's normal, I think," he said. "You know, go to college, get married, and build a career, a family, and a lifestyle. But my 'second life' is about how the whole package gets used for your benefit, yes, but also for the benefit of others."

To that end, Glenn has become an ambassador for the University of Massachusetts, putting together leadership programs for alumni and others where a diverse group of speakers and guests share their own experiences to inspire and instruct others. He is a trusted advisor to UMass's president, Jack Wilson, on a wide range of topics, and Glenn also has taken an active role in supporting stem-cell research. He is a frequent motivational speaker himself, and his topics range from leading others under adverse circumstances to the power of resilience and people's ability to "push the edge of possibility" beyond what we think we are capable of achieving.

"For me, I realized my brain still worked, even if my legs didn't," he said.

Wow. Read that over a few times the next time you think your situation is so unbearable and the breaks aren't going your way—it puts your bad-hair day or your rotten luck into proper perspective, doesn't it? Even if you feel as though you lost something as a result of your trigger event, even if it feels like you lost everything, you still have so much left. Glenn's attitude is exactly what I have been stressing throughout your time on my team. He exemplifies it and so much more.

When I reflect on Glenn's story, I'm reminded of the quote from one of the most inspiring movies I've ever seen, *The Shawshank Redemption*. In the scene where Andy Dufresne (Tim Robbins) tells Red (Morgan Freeman), "I guess it comes down to a simple choice, really. Get busy living, or get busy dying."

Glenn got busy living, and that's what I'm asking out of you in your own "second life."

"The new me," Glenn said, "is driven and fearless—[to the point] where sometimes I feel invincible. When I see an opportunity to participate, I don't ask for permission; I just jump right in. I say to myself, *What's the worst that could happen? I've already discovered a deep bottom, and I'm okay.*"

I'd say Glenn is more than okay, and it's further proof that you will be as well. **Glenn's story teaches us all to not waste time regretting the old ending, but to be grateful for the new beginning.**

> **PractiCal Point:** Take stock of all the good and bad parts of your first life and keep only the best aspects as you begin your second life.

· · ·

I realize your own bounce-back reentry probably won't include a press conference televised live locally and national stories being written about you. But at Memphis mine did, and while the pressure that comes from that sort of attention may seem overwhelming, it is nothing compared to the pressure I put on myself. I don't think it's a bad thing to be your own harshest critic as long as you stay realistic about the goals you have set.

"This is not going to be easy," I told the assembled media and supporters on March 11, 2000. "This is not like, 'Let's just waltz to the Final Four.' This is a challenge, but I get excited about these kinds of challenges."

Once the pomp and circumstance of my introductory press conference was over and I had the chance to launch *my* brand to the Tiger faithful, it was time to roll up our sleeves and start to get the lay of the land.

I apologized in advance to community leaders and university officials by explaining I would be largely inaccessible during my first couple of weeks. I told everyone I felt the first week to ten days on the job were the most important, and I believe that is the case for you during your bounce back as well.

My priorities started with recruiting—you'll recall how important recruiting is in college athletics—and simultaneously included getting a staff together that would be persistent in recruiting and unrelenting in helping me create the love affair with the city of Memphis.

You, too, need to get your priorities in order; write them down, edit them, and stick to that list. It makes no difference if it's a new job you are entering or a new relationship, you need to look within yourself and determine what it is you want to accomplish in the first week, the first month, the first sixty days, and so on.

Here are some of the themes I worked with during my first month at Memphis.

1. Get early "wins"

Regardless of what new adventure you are beginning, nothing will instill confidence in yourself and those around you better than quick and clear victories. Even the seemingly small endeavors will begin to build momentum for you. For instance, if you're in the early stages of a new relationship, give your significant other one of those corny (or humorous) greeting cards, and write something sweet, displaying how happy you are to have that person in your life. It could also be something as simple as a single red rose or breakfast in bed. Not only will it make your partner smile, it will boost your own self-esteem, reassuring yourself you have the ability to love someone else.

As a leader, your peers want to know you care about them and understand their personal needs. When you are building a winning attitude in a company or in yourself, you need to be consistent and dedicated to the vision you have laid out.

2. It's the people, stupid!

James Carville coined the popular phrase "It's the economy, stupid" during the 1992 presidential campaign. For all of us during our bounce backs, it's more about the people than the money. It's not the bricks and mortar; it's the human beings who make the difference. The first most important thing during this stage of your bounce back is to surround yourself with good people who are talented and committed to whatever cause you are venturing into. I learned early on in my career that the most important ingredient to success was hiring good people. The second most important thing is for you to project the best image of yourself to everyone you know; you never know when you'll have a chance to impress the right person who can launch you forward. Pat Nardelli, a good friend and successful real estate developer in Pittsburgh, once told me, **"You can have a bad deal with good people—things happen—but you can never have a good deal with bad people."**

3. Listen twice as much as you talk

I've mentioned this before, but it's even more important to focus on now that you have entered the reintroduction phase of your bounce back.

You've probably heard the oft-repeated quote, "There is a reason you have two ears and one mouth." I love that, and I think there's a valuable lesson to be learned from it for us all.

Further down the road, these strategies, along with your hard work and good attitude, are going to gradually make you an indispensable part of whatever organization or relationship you find yourself a part of. The concept of indispensability is one that needs time to evolve, but it's one you need to start from Day One of your second life.

On the court, we call it doing the "dirty work"—setting a screen, deflecting a pass, tipping a rebound to a teammate. Those are all "hustle points," and my players take pride in doing those mostly unnoticed chores that lead to winning. For you, the hustle points will be getting in early to your office and staying late, completing tasks before deadline, and being available for any extra work. Or if you're building a relationship, it may mean doing the laundry the day before your spouse usually does it just to give him or her the day off. Any number of small things soon add up to noticeable efforts that inevitably impress those around you.

Want to know how you'll recognize when it is that you have become indispensable? Well, if you're at a new job, there will be a night when you get food poisoning or some nasty twenty-four-hour bug, and no matter how hard you try to get out of bed and shower and get to the office, you just can't do it.

When you wake up around noon feeling a tiny bit better, you have five voice mails and eight text messages, and every one of them is asking, "Where are you? Is everything okay? We're all worried sick about you."

That is when you have become indispensable. Now, if you get that same food poisoning or flu and stay in bed for three days and no one—not even the interns—calls to see how you're doing or emails you with a question, you pretty much know you are dispensable!

When that indispensability is reached, it's a sign that your hard work and your commitment is paying off and that a promotion, a raise, or a unique opportunity is coming your way—all because you were willing to work past exhaustion.

> **PractiCal Point:** Make yourself indispensable by doing the dirty work, and watch the doors it opens for you in your bounce back. Be as positive and as motivational as you can—leave an impression on everyone you encounter.

• • •

I don't want this to sound like an episode of *Extreme Makeover Home Edition,* but the point is, we had to step everything up to let people know right away we would not settle for anything but top-notch at Memphis. You can wait for the ship to come to dock, or you can swim out to meet it. There was too much at stake, so we swam out!

It would have been easy to come in and make all sorts of demands and throw my weight around to get what we needed. But that's no way to enter a new situation, and you better keep it in mind during your first few months in your bounce-back opportunity. Instead, what I did was, I had informal, relaxed conversations with university officials and community leaders. I wasn't concerned with letting people hear what I knew; I instead wanted to find out what they knew.

You, too, need to take this approach. Find the veterans in the organization, and pepper them with questions. Get a feel for where you fit in this new position you have earned. If you're smart, you'll be able to learn a lot about the organization that will be important for you as you grow there. You'll learn the history of the place, and you might even start hearing about problems that need to be fixed that you can keep your eye on. Most important, you'll show people that you are invested in the organization that they're a part of. **People don't care what you know until they know you care.**

> **PractiCal Point:** Look under the rug, but don't start sweeping until you have had time to get input from those who have institutional knowledge of the situation.

PRACTICE PLAN #6

SECOND-LIFE

EMPHASIS OF THE DAY: Establish good habits for your "second life."

"Habit," said educator Horace Mann, "is a cable; we weave a thread of it each day, and at last we cannot break it."

The problem with that is, if we are entwining the cable with "bad" threads, the cable can become a noose. The bad habits will wreck your life, they will knock your knees out from under you, but the good ones will define not just your bounce back but your second life as well.

Like you, I always had habits or routines prior to my trigger event. Some were as mundane as getting my Dunkin' Donuts coffee in the morning, and others were as important as always having a meeting with my UMass and Nets staffs each and every day to be sure we were all on the same page.

PURPOSE

Making good habits a fundamental part of your bounce back will set you up for success in your reentry opportunity and pave the way for a smooth road ahead. With this drill I'm going to ask you to examine the habits—good and bad—from your first life and write them down on one sheet of paper. When that is completed, I want you to make a list of the habits you are going to make a concerted effort to maintain from now on and forever.

The habits can be physical, mental, or both. They can involve your workout regimen or the amount of time each day you will spend reaching out to your loved ones. You can carry over all or some of the good ones from your first life, but whatever they are, be sure they are habits you can reasonably maintain, and don't allow them to have any resemblance to the bad ones you listed.

Like all of our Practice Plans, you will want to save this one and look back on it frequently in the coming days, months, and years.

DRILL

FIRST LIFE

Bad habits (health, lifestyle, work, social, etc.) I had:

SECOND LIFE

Good habits I will strive for:

WATCH ME FIRST

How I perceive the difference between my "first life" until the Nets firing and my "second life" since that PractiCal Point:

FIRST LIFE

Bad habits (health, lifestyle, work, social, etc.) I had:

   Getting bogged down in minutiae

   Spreading myself too thin

   Not being able to say no

   Neglecting nutrition and exercise at certain points

SECOND LIFE

Good habits (health, lifestyle, work, social, etc.) I will strive for:

    Work ethic

    Building and maintaining relationships

    Helping others and taking joy from that

    Appreciating the moment and living in it

    Focusing on exercise and nutrition

CHAPTER 12

KNUCKLE BALLS, MEGA MOUNTAINS, AND CRATERS

DON'T LET BUMPS IN THE ROAD
DETOUR YOU

L et's not be naive; those first days, weeks, and months of my own "second life" at Memphis were filled with triumphs and tribulations, forward progress and backward slips. I wouldn't have it any other way, to be honest.

I've never believed achieving success was just about working hard; if that were the case, there'd be a heck of a lot more successful people in every walk of life. Hard work is just one part of the winning equation. You must enjoy the hard work you are putting in so you can develop that swagger and confidence we talked about earlier. Hard work without passion is like walking through wet cement. **You need to learn to love the path to the prize as much as the prize itself.**

Our game plan at Memphis was to build a national program, graduate our student-athletes, play in front of sold-out crowds on national television, and compete for national titles. Those are attainable goals for any top-level program, but at the time I was committing to them upon my hiring in Memphis, they were lofty as well. And there was no way that they would be achieved overnight.

So when our first game at Memphis finally rolled around on the night of November 17, 2000, it signaled a return to normalcy for me. Even the opponent was a familiar one for both me and my staff—Temple University. Tony Barbee, Derek Kellogg, and our Minutemen teams had been through some epic battles with the Owls and Coach John Chaney when we were all at UMass. Temple had owned UMass during the history of the series, winning the first twenty-one straight, and I started with eight consecutive losses against Coach Chaney before we were able to turn the tide and begin our run of five straight Atlantic 10 titles (in both regular season and the league tournament).

The university's marketing department had been distributing buttons and bumper stickers proclaiming, IT's BACK. For sure, something was back in Memphis, and it was being welcomed with open arms and screaming lungs.

Having ESPN there raised the excitement to another level as nearly twenty thousand fans packed The Pyramid. Ticket scalpers reappeared for the first time in many years outside the arena. Fans painted their faces, wore blue and white, and held signs that read MEMPHIS IS CALIPARI COUNTRY and the TV-camera-friendly EVERYBODY'S SCARED TO PLAY US NOW. The Memphis mascot at the time, Tom II—a live, caged Bengal tiger—roared from his courtside perch, only adding to the circuslike atmosphere. It was unbelievable; it really was.

That first night it seemed as though the whole city had just been waiting for something to rally around, and we were going to be that focal point. Unfortunately, we weren't quite ready for a starring role. We wound up losing, 67–62. Temple was too poised and too confident for us. We just weren't at their level yet.

We were 1–3 at Thanksgiving. The only thing I was thankful for was that we weren't 0–4! We went on to lose five of our next eight and sat at 4–8 as December wound down. It was a less-than-auspicious beginning, and I'd be lying if I said I didn't have doubts, concerns, and more than a little bit of anxiety.

But you know what? That's all part of the process. This thing was going to take time and patience—the same way your bounce back has required those vital qualities.

Even at the stage you're at now, no one is promising your new situation is going to be a bed of roses. In fact, I can promise you it won't be. But you have become so strong and so resilient in getting to this point that there is no way you will let early setbacks undermine your overall goals. **You can't let *any* setbacks deter you from living out the bounce-back story you have written.**

I compare this phase of your bounce back to working out at the gym. There is a lot of repetition, and you might not always notice the changes right away. But you feel best at the end of a workout when you have pushed yourself to exhaustion. You bust through the pain and go far beyond what you thought your limits were.

Every part of your body is soaked in perspiration as are your T-shirt, your shorts, your socks. The sweat rolls off your nose, and you puff in and out, over and over again. You have to peel everything off your body, and the pile you create at your feet on the locker-room floor leaves a sweat stain.

Those days—with your body tingling, when you get into the shower or the steam room and feel like you couldn't give one more ounce of energy—are the days that bring you the greatest satisfaction. It's those mornings-after, when you wake up sore but renewed, that convince you that you're working to your full potential.

Are you willing to work to exhaustion? Will you find that tingly

feeling? That's my job as a basketball coach—to get my players working to exhaustion and feeling good about it. As your coach, I know
you, too, can fight the fatigue and flourish—you've already proven it
over the course of our training together. When you do achieve that
natural high, you will have the option of saying, "I hate it" or "I love
it." I'm telling you, you're going to love it, and when you do, tomorrow you'll try to get that exact same feeling back, and the next day
and the next day and . . .

> **PractiCal Point:** Be prepared for early setbacks, and use those
> experiences to bolster every aspect of your bounce back.

• • •

In these initial days of your bounce-back opportunity you need to be
hyperaware of everything going on within you and around you. Trust
your gut, but also lean on some of the same people you leaned on to get
here. I remember talking to my Kitchen Cabinet members—especially
Coach Brown, Bob Marcum, and Bruiser Flint—consistently as we slid
down the slippery slope to 4–8. You've got to understand something:
I had only one losing season in my time at UMass (our first year in
1988–89, when we finished 10–18). In my final five years in Amherst
we didn't lose eight games in a season even once.

It wasn't a surprise, then, that I began doubting myself and our
system. You can't do that, though, as hard as it may seem, because
through all the debris of your turnaround, it's your "system" that you
have to believe in most.

We skidded a little bit toward the end of the regular season, dropping four of our last six, but by the time postseason came, we were a

much-improved team and earned an invitation to the National Invitation Tournament, advancing to the semifinals in Madison Square Garden and finishing 21–15.

It was in the middle of that first season when I encountered what I would consider the first curveball of my reentry opportunity. More accurately, this one was a vintage Phil "Knucksie" Niekro knuckleball that floated, danced, and sank right at my feet. There are going to be all kinds of unexpected snafus and twists in your bounce back, and I want you to be prepared for them, not overreact, and rationally think of ways to make the best out of what you may initially deem a bad situation.

In mid-January of 2001, a group of Memphis's business leaders asked to have a meeting with me in my office to discuss a project they were working on. I was thinking, *Great, these people want to get behind the team and support us.*

I came to find out the group wasn't actually there to offer support; they were there to offer competition. Memphis had long been trying to land a professional sports team, mostly focusing on an NFL franchise. The city was snubbed time and time again, and Memphians were skeptical of ever getting a professional organization to the Bluff City. The group I met with that day was quite a bit more optimistic. Brothers Staley and Andy Cates, Marty Regan, and Gayle Rose were part of a supersecret "pursuit team" dedicated to attracting an NBA club to Memphis. Their plans had been kept under tight wraps, and Gayle, one of Memphis's most philanthropically minded leaders, later admitted how nervous they were to talk to anyone outside of the inner circle while working on the plans.

They made a presentation to me, emphasizing what a boon an NBA franchise would be to the city, how it would increase Memphis's profile, and how they would use the team to foster charitable events and community outreach throughout the city. They didn't know when or if a team would become available or when a relocation of an existing club would be possible, but they wanted to be fully prepared when it did happen. (There were eventually two options, with Vancouver ultimately winding up in Memphis.)

The group had obviously done their homework, and after I got over the initial shock of what they were proposing, I was able to look at their dream and constructively figure out how it would affect our program.

Marty Regan, an attorney, would later tell the *Commercial Appeal,* "It would have died right there if [John] had said, 'I came to Memphis with the idea that I would have the biggest game in town, and I view that as detrimental to the department and to sports here.'"

Throughout our meeting they continued to emphasize that they would only move forward if I was on board with the idea. That meant a lot to me. But I still had to think it over. Initially I could only see how tough this would make my job. Here I was trying to build a love affair with the city, and these folks wanted to bring in a blond bombshell to distract everyone's attention from the Tigers. That worried me.

I was concerned about how having an NBA franchise would affect our fund-raising and ticket sales. But I knew that as long as we took care of business with the Tigers and made progress each year, the fans would latch onto and embrace our program.

Selfishly, I admit, I was cognizant of the fact that once an NBA team came to town, my endorsement opportunities would be depleted. It's okay to be selfish once in a while, especially when it comes to competition—you have earned the position you are in and deserve good things. At that point I was the only real sports celebrity in town, and I was able to pick and choose carefully what deals I entered into. With NBA players and coaches coming to town, the pie would be divided up a bit more.

As a program, we would have to share the sports page and TV and radio coverage. But I realized that, too, was okay, because it would mean some of our regional rivals like Tennessee, Mississippi, and Arkansas would get bumped further back in the papers and newscasts. That was a good thing.

I saw other benefits too: recruiting to a "pro" city would be an advantage we never had at UMass; having pro scouts in town for an NBA game would mean unlimited opportunities for our players to be seen by NBA decision makers—that would be great exposure for our guys and another valuable recruiting tool; there would also have to be a new arena built, and it was likely we would share that building.

The more time I spent assessing the pluses and minuses, the more comfortable I became with the proposition. I reasoned that in order to get our love affair with the city rolling, we needed as many people falling in love with the sport of basketball as possible; more buzz about the roundball would mean more chances to hook the fans.

I looked at the bigger picture and thought as long as we were made whole, as long as they were looking after our interests—which they stressed in that first meeting—it would be another thing to raise the image of the city. Anything that helped the city, I concluded, would help the program. Many disagreed with me, but it proved to be true.

That whole situation—in the middle of my first season, no less— could have been a disaster, especially if I had become unreasonable or stubborn. I do believe the group would have stopped their pursuit, but I also know it would have made me more enemies than friends, and that's no way to start off a new relationship. I think the smartest thing I did was listen to their proposition and give myself plenty of time to think about it. I didn't react in the room when the group made the presentation. I talked to as many people as I could, people whom I knew would be affected by the decision before making a judgment on what I thought was best.

The NBA group's desires caught me off guard, I'll say that. In any new environment, there are going to be outside distractions and details to deal with.

You need to realize that in your bounce back the most important thing you can bring to a new opportunity is an open mind. Be aware of this very type of situation where you are thrown a curveball early in your new experience. Do not automatically dismiss an idea, a venture, or a direction you disagree with. There's positive possibility in almost every situation you encounter. Take some time to look at all the factors, as I did with the NBA proposition, and then make an informed, intelligent decision.

As a coach, I learned so much from that first Memphis team and everything that season encompassed. I realized first and foremost that my own bounce back was a work in progress. I knew that my confidence wasn't all the way back yet; I was sometimes coaching to not lose instead of to win. That's hard to admit when it's happening, but you know if it is the case. It's totally normal. It's hard for anyone to take responsibility; the natural reaction is to blame others and point to what should have been. *It was the players I had. It was the schedule we played. It was the practice facilities being subpar.* But you know what? In the end, all of it was on no one but me. There was no need to focus energy on any other excuses, reasons, or explanations.

Do not, under any circumstance, allow yourself to play the blame game. You work with what you are given, and you make the most out of it—always.

That 2000–01 team could have given up; they could have blamed the coaching change, the new demands, the new uniforms, whatever. But they didn't as players and we didn't as a staff. The team would listen and eventually understand, as long as we led them down the right road and built their trust in us.

To everyone's credit, we all stuck together and realized we had enough talent to become a good team once we figured out the best way to play. It was, in retrospect, a crucial, foundation-building season. We got the program back to the postseason, we gave fans something to cling to, and we began to build our new brand identity.

Our following season I thought we were good enough to make the NCAA Tournament, especially because we had the highly touted freshman Dajuan Wagner as part of my first full recruiting class. If not for a late-season slide and a first-round exit from the Conference USA tournament, we would have broken through to the Big Dance. As it was, we won twenty-seven games, the most for the school in more than fifteen years. We were able to bounce back from the letdown of not making the NCAA Tournament, and we won our last five straight to earn the NIT Championship at MSG.

I was seeing progress in almost everything we were doing—sometimes I had to look hard to find it, but I know if you examine your situation, you, too, will be able to see progress. Use that progress as stepping stones to get you to where you want to be—and don't let "the miserables" cloud your vision.

In two seasons we had gone 48–24, reached postseason play twice, and were clearly heading in the right direction. But for some fans and media in Memphis, it wasn't enough. For Sale signs started popping up randomly on my front lawn, some kind of message from disgruntled fans who wanted me to know that I wasn't meeting their expectations. I kept a few of those signs in my Memphis garage as a reminder of how fleeting success is and how fickle people can be.

Those signs were a constant reminder that we weren't just climbing a mountain; we were scaling Mount Everest.

Truth be told, where we were after year two wasn't enough for me either. Like I said, there is no one harder on me than me, and it will always be that way. If you're that way, remember that it's okay to be ambitious and to push yourself hard; you just can't be too discouraged if things take you longer than you expected.

> **PractiCal Point:** Notice the lessons you are learning during every step of your bounce back; take the time to understand these lessons.

. . .

One of my biggest priorities in the early years at Memphis was to not just have good teams, but to build a solid *program*. There's a big difference, and any successful business leader knows exactly what I'm talking about. Do you want to be a one-hit wonder, or do you want to be in it for the long haul? My philosophy in rebuilding brands is to never trim corners or skip steps. Adopt that same attitude, and you will be putting yourself in the best position to prosper.

This is why I always put a huge emphasis on recruiting and why I constantly want the best, brightest, and most connected assistants on my staff to foster relationships and build trust with the young men we want to bring into our program. I know that having Dajuan Wagner at Memphis—even for just the one year—was going to help our future recruiting in immeasurable ways. When "Juanny" came to our program, it made it cool to be a Tiger. We began to get involved with more and more elite-level players soon after. But that, too, had its own downside; we wound up losing out on some of our marquee signees when (now-perennial NBA All-Star) Amar'e Stoudemire and Qyntel Woods went directly into the 2002 NBA draft. (It wasn't until 2006 that the NBA mandated players be at least one year removed from high school—and nineteen years old—in order to enter the draft.) The following year we had a commitment from Kendrick Perkins, but he also entered the draft, where he was selected twenty-seventh by the Memphis Grizzlies then traded to Boston, where he wound up being a key contributor to the Celtics championship team in 2007–08.

Obviously, our timetable would have been accelerated greatly if we were able to keep all three of those first-round NBA picks, but, trust me, no one wants to hear what could have been. Wouldas, couldas, and shouldas don't go over too well in any walk of life or business. We never used it as an excuse because we knew full well there was the chance those players would skip college altogether. They were so good, we were willing to take that chance.

I share that particular anecdote with you to show you the necessity of persisting through setbacks within all areas of your bounce back. As tough as it was to lose kids to the NBA, it was also an indication that we were getting involved with the very best of the best. It was something we could use to our advantage in recruiting, and we did. I kept reminding myself through those first few years that it isn't about winning each time out—although that's a tremendous bonus—but it's about *learning* each time out. Whether it's a game, a recruit, a business deal, or a date, you need to constantly be taking lessons from each experience.

We all know innately we won't "win" every time, no matter what the challenge may be, so we must prepare ourselves to "lose" every now and again. Working with great confidence toward a dream and having blind faith puts you on that path to success; by staying on that path you will be able to see failure as your next building block instead of stumbling block.

I did what I would ask you to do if you are experiencing some snafus or doubts within your bounce back: look at your past and see how things progressed for you in similar situations before. I think you'll find that even your most ideal jobs and relationships went through some rough waters before finding smooth sailing. The human mind tends to only remember the good things when it is mourning a lost relationship or career opportunity. I'm telling you, you also endured some not-so-great things and were able to recover from them.

I often find myself thinking back to another impediment to our progress during our time at Memphis. This one, which came during the 2005–06 season, wasn't merely a bump in the road—it was a crater.

In January of the prior season, Jeremy Hunt, a Memphis native and a junior at the time, was involved in a shameful situation where he was arrested on charges of misdemeanor assault on a former girlfriend, who played on the Tigers women's team. Jeremy was suspended for two games by the university, and I put him on notice—in no uncertain terms—that he was on the shortest of leashes. It was zero tolerance time for Jeremy, and I was once again thinking I could be Father Flanagan.

When the fall 2005 semester began, Jeremy was involved in an altercation on Beale Street witnessed by several people, and soon enough the fight was front-page news in the city.

When Jeremy's Beale Street brawl was brought to light, I kicked him off the team. The university and I had gone out of our way to give Jeremy every chance to be a part of our program (and he had been through his share of injuries as well), but we could not allow his actions to continue to be an ongoing distraction for our team, our program, and our university. I regretted having to cut him loose—I had only done that one time before, at UMass with Mike Williams—but it was in the best interest of our program.

I had to look past Jeremy the basketball player—he was never a regular starter for us in his first three years, but he managed to average better than nine points per game—and look at Jeremy the person and make sure I was giving him the best opportunity to learn and grow from his repeated mistakes. I left Jeremy's scholarship open for him, and I told him he needed to finish his degree, because there were no guarantees that basketball would take care of him forever.

Jeremy was popular among his teammates, and his dismissal could have been devastating to what we hoped to accomplish that season. But here's the thing I want you to take out of the circumstances of Jeremy's regrettable decisions: I was able to take what was a crisis for our team at the time and actually turn it into a unifying moment for our program.

Jeremy wound up earning his bachelor's degree in University College/African American Community and Sports Education. While doing so, he still attended games and made every effort to turn his life around. In early summer of 2006, he asked for a review of his standing with the team.

At first I was shocked and almost dismissive of the idea. How could we trust him not to embarrass the program again? We had said at the time it was a "permanent dismissal," and going back on that had potential to be a PR nightmare for me and the university.

Then I met with Jeremy, and what I saw was a young man who had been humbled and who had truly changed his ways. The great thing was that Jeremy's mother, Gloria, had supported everything we had done with Jeremy. She kept telling me, "He made his own bed and now has got to sleep in it." In addition to being a teacher and brutally honest, Gloria's a very strong and influential woman in Jeremy's life. Knowing we had her in our corner added a level of security in believing what Jeremy was saying.

For the year he was not on the team he did all the right things and everything we asked of him.

"Coach," he had written in a letter to me, "it killed me to watch from the stands as my teammates were having so much fun. I will accept whatever role you have for me on the court. More important, Coach, I have changed. What happened to me was my own doing, and I take responsibility for that. You will not have to worry about me again."

If you understand anything about me after reading this book, you know that I believe in second chances and redemption stories. Jeremy had absolutely made mistakes, but I could see that he had really learned from them and believed in himself enough to ask for a second chance. This was an important step in his own bounce back, and I wanted to show him that he could be rewarded for taking responsibility for himself and his life. Sometimes, in order to change behavior, there needs to be a crisis, be it big or small. Jeremy went through a major crisis of self-discovery.

I guess I open myself to criticism with my forgiving nature, but I am both an educator and a coach, and life lessons are a big part of what I always need to be teaching the young men I coach. I can handle the slings and arrows that come my way.

Still, I told Jeremy this would be a tough thing to make happen, and I wasn't convinced it was the right thing to do. He had broken a promise with the Memphis president, Dr. Shirley Raines, the prior year, and in the end this was going to be her call.

In July I met with Dr. Raines, and she was shocked I was even broaching the topic. "He was permanently suspended, and in my opinion we have given him plenty of chances," Dr. Raines said. "What if he does something to embarrass our university again?"

Her point was well taken, and there was also the issue of having used the word *permanent* in the release announcing Jeremy's dismissal.

My answer to that was, let's not use semantics as a reason to affect this young man's life. If he merits being reinstated, then we should do it—press release be damned.

What I have always considered when making decisions like this is, "How would I want my son to be treated?" My answer is, I would want him to be punished as severely as necessary to get him to change the destructive behavior. If he changed, if he did everything asked of him, and if he showed remorse, I would then want some compassion shown.

About a week later, Dr. Raines called a meeting with me, Jeremy, and his mother. She told us Jeremy was going to have to agree to some very strict conditions and that if he stepped out of line *at all*, it would be over. Dr. Raines had faith in me as a coach and in Jeremy as a person and showed great compassion and thoughtfulness. We all cried and hugged in an emotional scene in her office when the decision was made. Jeremy was being given a bounce-back opportunity, and it was all on him to do what was right and provide a happy ending for his story.

Some people in the community were outraged, thinking I was putting basketball before all else. It was quite the contrary, actually, and I have never—not for one minute—regretted the decision to bring Jeremy back.

Jeremy became a leader for us on that team and had a career year, playing in all thirty-seven games and averaging 14.1 points per game. But it wasn't the basketball accomplishments that I'm most proud of (he plays over in Europe now and often visited when we were in Memphis); it's the strides he made in becoming a man that I always talk about when Jeremy's name is brought up.

I try to walk a hundred steps with a student before letting go of his hand. I'll take the bullets for being too compassionate or too lenient because I know that in ten, twenty, or fifty years that decision will not be remembered. What will be remembered is that a young man like Jeremy got a chance to turn his life around—to bounce back from a situation he created entirely by himself—and took advantage of that opportunity.

> **PractiCal Point:** Allow the crises of the past and interruptions in your progress to become unifying events and personal growth opportunities.

CHAPTER 13

PLAN YOUR WORK, WORK YOUR PLAN

INNOVATE AND EXPERIMENT
WHEN YOU ARE PREPARED TO RISK IT ALL

After those initial months you will find yourself at a point in your bounce back where you are comfortable enough to begin experimenting and innovating. Don't rush to get to this juncture—you will know when the time is right.

For me, it was a gradual process and didn't begin to unfold until my fourth season in Memphis, and even then it took two more years to get to a point where I was ready to take a substantial risk.

Going back to my UMass days, I've always encouraged coaches to visit my teams' practices. I don't care if they're at the high-school, junior-college, or CYO level; I believe we all need to help one another, share ideas, and spread the game of basketball to all corners of the earth. It's corny to say, but I want to give back to the game that has given me so much in my life.

Vance Walberg was one such coach who visited us for three days in October 2003. He was beginning his first season as head coach at Fresno City College, and he had always made time to tour the country and visit with the best and brightest in college basketball. In the years before we met, he had watched the practices of, and discussed basketball with, a host of the game's best, from Dean Smith to Bobby Knight to Billy Donovan.

On Vance's second night in town we went out to eat in Memphis. As is my habit, we talked basketball throughout the meal, and I really enjoyed spending time with Vance—he was a true Basketball Benny, a student of the game who ate, drank, and slept Dr. Naismith's invention. Once the meal was finished, my curiosity got the better of me, and I asked Vance what kind of offense he was going to be running in his first year at Fresno City. I'm always fascinated by listening to what others are doing to either innovate or improve on old principles.

I'll never forget his answer: "You don't want to know," he laughed. "It's a little bit off the wall."

I insisted, and in no time Vance had cleared space and created a "court" on our table. Salt shakers were baskets and sugar packets were players.

Now you've got to understand, I had always been a fairly old-school coach when it came to offense (and defense too). I believed in play-calling from the bench and running the classic motion offense, based mainly on screening (setting picks).

I wasn't necessarily looking to change what I was doing, because, to be honest, I was having pretty good success doing it my way. But I always wanted to be aware of what others were trying and seeing if any of their concepts would fit with what I was doing or if I would be able to game plan against it.

Vance's offense blew me away. It gave every player the freedom to take his man to the hoop on every play. I saw it as something that would unleash players and could potentially be a huge recruiting tool because of its up-tempo, frenetic pace. Scoring opportunities would be plentiful, and it was like nothing I've ever seen put into action. Let's face it, every kid wants to put up scoring numbers, and in this offense Vance was showing me, every kid could.

This creation of his *was* out there for sure; it was unconventional in every way. There was very little screening, tons of quick shots, and penetration at all opportunities, and it allowed for unlimited three-point shots. It was so outrageous I was oddly intrigued by it. I began to talk to Vance on the phone frequently. I tested bits and pieces of it and often debated its merits with my assistants and coaching peers.

I'm not afraid to change, nor am I afraid to do things differently, but I will never just jump into something without thoroughly investigating it.

Two years later after hundreds of phone calls to Vance and multiple trips to Fresno to watch his team practice, I was comfortable enough to install the offense at Memphis. I never could have envisioned the success my teams have had with the offense—which I have tweaked and adapted.

Just about everyone I ran the offense by was skeptical, if not downright opposed to it. Coach Brown—who has since come around to it—told me, "You've won hundreds of games playing a certain way, and now you're going to change? And it's a junior-college coach from California? What are you, crazy?"

When I first met Vance (whose son Jason is now on my Kentucky staff), I wasn't in the driveway of crazy yet, but I was roaming the neighborhood. Eventually I bought the house. When I began using the Dribble Drive Motion (DDM) with my program, it felt like I'd been a teacher with the same lesson plan for fifteen years—the one that never changed—the one brothers and sisters all remembered being taught.

The motion offense I'd been running wasn't necessarily a bad lesson plan, but it was getting moldy and musty. Making the switch to DDM reinvigorated me because it got me to rethink the game and to study it anew. It challenged me as a coach and as a teacher. The kids really took to it; despite the fact that it took a while for most to truly understand it, they all rave about it once it's being run at an optimum level—it challenges them, but it also prepares them for most anything they will see on the court.

You need to be exploring a new neighborhood in your bounce back as well. I can assure you if you choose carefully, it will have the same energizing effect on you as Vance's system has had on me and our teams.

The important part of this story is twofold: First, I was open to new ideas. How many times have you heard coworkers, friends, or family immediately shoot down an idea they deemed too radical? Resistance to change is not something that will help your bounce back. Second, even though I didn't implement the concepts of Vance's offense—which he called AASA (Attack, Attack, Skip, Attack) but I streamlined to DDM—I inched toward the point when I was comfortable enough in my new situation to take a significant risk. Whether you are currently there or wending your way to that point, when you are willing to risk it all, you will know your bounce back has reached another plateau.

All of this speaks to your ability to be inventive. It does *not* mean you abandon your operating system all together. Was it risky for me to ditch the comfort of a system that had given me more than three hundred college wins? I suppose it was. But that's not the way I was thinking at the time. I had done two solid years of research on Vance's innovation, and I had added enough of my own variations based on my personnel to put me in a comfort zone.

You have to continue to believe in your system and allow change to come about normally and at its own pace. If you see somebody executing a plan in a way that you admire, take your time to make sure that you really understand what they're doing before you apply it in your own life. You've got to make sure you know it inside and out before you can make it your own.

If there is any doubt in your own mind, then you need to hold off. I crawled into the DDM instead of sprinting into it. If I had gone in without my entire heart and soul, there was no way we would be having the success we have enjoyed with it. The kids would have seen through it, my staff would have been skeptical, and it would have been a disaster if I wasn't completely committed to the radical change.

So when I reached the point where I was in my comfort zone, it simply became a matter of teaching and implementing something I believed in wholeheartedly.

> **PractiCal Point:** Tinker and experiment
> to bring about incredible results—just be
> sure to proceed with caution.

• • •

There were definitely other monkey wrenches thrown our way during the first two-thirds of our time in Memphis. Chief among them was probably the 2004–05 season. That was the year when Darius missed his free throws against Louisville in the Conference USA title game, keeping us out of an automatic bid to the NCAA Tournament. Even though we went to the Final Four of the postseason NIT, we finished at 22–16, the most single-season losses of my Memphis tenure. I wasn't brought to the Bluff City to get NIT trophies; I was hired to hang NCAA banners, and I knew it. That season was probably the biggest setback I experienced in my bounce-back reentry opportunity, and, believe me, it hurt like a son of a gun.

More of those "For Sale" signs starting popping up on our front lawn, and the message boards were alive with suggestions that I wasn't the right guy for the job. Media began to question what I was doing. There was doubt and leeriness from almost all corners. I even think my dog, Dash, might have stopped coming near me!

It wasn't that I had failed altogether—we were still making progress in the areas of marketing and ticket sales, and our kids were focusing on their studies as we demanded. But the bottom line was that we were not winning enough. Even with our shared vision of excellence and with the benefit of hard work, the results just weren't there.

There could very well be moments like this in your own bounce back, and, again, I want you to know how I handled my setbacks so you can be better informed when you run into complications.

At this time in your bounce back, some people will scatter, and others will hunker down. Believe me, it would have been easy to succumb to all the negativity. But I never did. I know the people who scattered—"the miserables"—had never fully bought in, and the ones who hunkered down recognized that failures have to come before successes.

The way I judge the people I work with and the players I coach is by something I call the "Ammo Test." If we were in a bunker together and the crap hit the fan, with bullets and shrapnel flying furiously, would I be comfortable sending someone for more ammunition?

That decision would be based on knowing whether the person would return. To win a championship, the people you are with—and the people above you as well—must be completely faithful to the cause. They have to be willing to go get the ammo and have the fortitude to come back. As frustrated as I was in that situation, it was my job to keep thinking about the future and show the people around me that good things would be coming our way soon. It was the job of the people around me to put their faith in what I was saying and support us any way that they could.

You very well may have to deal with a similar fish-or-cut-bait instance in your own bounce back. I'm telling you to get that pole, cast another line, and continue trying to land the big one. The best thing I can tell you about this kind of impediment is that **failure is almost never fatal, nor is it ever final—unless you let it be.**

You know what I did the day after our season ended on March 29, 2005? I got right back to recruiting. Then I started writing thank-you notes to all our tremendous supporters for all they did for us throughout the season. I had year-end meetings with all our players and my staff. Then I went to St. Louis for the Final Four and saw all my old friends and basketball cronies. In other words, I acted as if everything was going smoothly and we were right on course.

What would it have looked like if I had gone into hibernation at that point? People would have been claiming I'd given up or that I was getting too old for the "young man's" game of recruiting. You better believe that season motivated me even more. I was going to work harder and more passionately that off-season than I had in all my previous off-seasons combined.

I even drew inspiration from Darius for the way he handled his missed free throws. He was told by more than a few people not to let two shots have a detrimental effect on his future. **"Don't let it break you; let it make you"** was the message Darius received over and over again.

I loved it. It's great advice for all of us at any stage of our bounce backs. If it doesn't kill you, it will make you stronger, and that's what I vowed the 2004–05 season would do for our program. That attitude had to begin at the top, with me, and filter through our whole organization.

For sure, things were swirling a bit, and as I said earlier, I'm at my best when there is some turmoil and tumult around me. Bruiser Flint always tells me I seem to pay more attention to detail when we're in the thick of it. Bru's right; those factors have a weird way of boosting my confidence and pushing me to prove the doubters wrong.

> **PractiCal Point:** Get by the anxiety, get by the fear, and then there is courage. You can't be afraid to make a mistake—I tell my players, "Just go play."

PRACTICE PLAN #7

MAKE A CLEAR AND CONCISE PATH FOR YOUR IMMEDIATE FUTURE

EMPHASIS OF THE DAY: Map out your plans for the first months of your reentry opportunity.

PURPOSE

There are some steps you will need to take in order to maximize all the efforts you have made to achieve your new opportunity. If some of these steps sound familiar to you, it's because I asked you to go through many similar drills during previous stages of your comeback. The common sense, calculated approach that made sense then makes sense once again. Now you have the added benefit of knowing these guidelines truly work. Set attainable but ambitious goals for the first few months of your reentry opportunity, and work to make them a reality. I viewed my first ninety days at Kentucky as the most important when I took the job in April 2009. Those first thirty days set us on the path we needed to be on, and over the next sixty days, we implemented the mechanism for success that will lead us to our goals.

DRILL

It's now time to focus your goals into actions and start devising a list of the steps you will use to attain them. In business circles, this is considered part of the onboarding process. Simply put, it's a way to pin down what new hires envision accomplishing in the first months at a new job. Oftentimes, employers will also plot out what they would like accomplished by certain milestone dates, and bonuses may even be tied into reaching those goals.

This plan will be completed when you have determined your goals for the following intervals of your bounce back. All the while, keep in mind that you want to steer clear of mistakes you made at these stages prior to your trigger event.

Goals I will strive for in my reentry opportunity during the . . .

FIRST 30 DAYS

NEXT 30

FINAL 30

WATCH ME FIRST
(I reached out to career coach Bobbie LaPorte, who provided me with some tips on maximizing the early days of the new opportunity. I took those suggestions and applied them to a wide range of bounce backs, but again, it's very likely you will be looking to incorporate these techniques into a new work situation.)

FIRST 30 DAYS

• *Get to know people, never eat alone in the cafeteria or at your desk, and define your role. Are you a point guard who will lead the team and distribute the ball? Are you a pure shooter who will want the ball down the stretch? Or are you a do-it-all, dirty-work guy?*

• *Build relationships inside and outside your department with a representative cross-section so you can see how your peers handle situations and how you fit into the culture of your new workplace.*

• *Establish a set of expectations with your boss or significant other. Refer to that list frequently and* **communicate** *with everyone involved.*

NEXT 30

• *Be sure that you are living up to your job description or to your partner's hopes for your relationship. Overcommunicate during this time—don't assume anything in career, life, or love.*

• *If you've begun to get off track in any area, remedy that, and continue moving forward at a steady, even pace.*

• *Start looking for quick-win projects that you can take ownership over.*

• *Show your support of others, and foster a team spirit. Share in their achievements as if they were your own by celebrating the successes of others enthusiastically.*

FINAL 30

• *Use some of the quick wins we discussed earlier to show your value and emphasize that you are becoming indispensable.*

• *Take on assignments outside your immediate purview (time permitting) to both meet more people and to learn how other departments function.*

- *Put yourself out there. Whatever crisis you are coming back from, you need to put on a good front and make the effort to have human contact, especially in social settings like office parties, charity events, and networking functions. This will show a commitment beyond your nine-to-five obligations and will allow others to know you on a more personal level.*

CHAPTER 14

THE NEVER-ENDING
BOUNCE BACK

I'm ten years from my first trigger event with the Nets as I write this. A full decade has passed since that cleanup-crew guy at the old Miami Arena was looking up from a pile of cups, wrappers, and popcorn and shaking his head in sympathy for me.

In that time since, I've uprooted my family from the Northeast to the Mid-South and now to Lexington, Kentucky. I've coached conference champions and NBA lottery picks, and I've been two minutes and twelve seconds from cutting down the nets in the NCAA title game. I built amazing and meaningful relationships in Memphis, and we hopefully made an impact on the community we were a part of for nine basketball seasons. I'm now starting a new adventure at one of the most storied basketball programs in the country, and my first couple of months have proven what an amazing opportunity I have been blessed with. I am truly humbled.

You know what else I am? I'm still bouncing back. Every day since the Nets fired me and every one that follows for the rest of my life, I will be continuing to write sentences, paragraphs, and chapters of my own bounce-back story. I think people may have believed I was "back" when Memphis advanced to three straight Elite 8s. They definitely were under that impression when we got to the Final Four and the championship game. Now there are even more who are probably ready to officially close the book on my bounce back, after my having landed this dream job with the Wildcats.

You and I know better than that though. We know bounce backs never truly end, and even if you are in a comfortable position and have reached the majority of your goals, you are still obligated to continue running even after you break the tape at the finish line.

If you'll recall in my "preseason" letter to you, I mentioned there will be a time when you'll reach back on the ladder you have valiantly climbed and lend a hand to the person or people behind you. *Do not* be the one who climbs up the ladder, turns around, and brings the ladder up and walks off by himself, never looking back. *Do* be the one who climbs it, turns around, and helps as many folks as he can. **Be grateful, and display that gratefulness in every sector of your life.**

Now is that time. It's not even an option; it's what I need everyone on our team to do, because the only way our bounce-back community can grow and prosper is for it to become a family in every sense of the word. **Your bounce back *never* ends.** The minute you think you are "back" and allow that mentality to seep into your consciousness, you are embracing fool's gold. **When you show your care and compassion for others you will be reminding yourself to never take anything for granted.**

There is no doubt in my mind that you have people around you— probably in your inner circle—who need to be guided, however gently, by the lessons and experiences you have gathered during your own personal bounce back. They might even be the same people you relied on so heavily at the beginning of your bounce back; as I said, things can change fast.

I have seen the benefits of giving back to others firsthand in an annual gathering Larry Brown and I started in 2002. The concept for the "Larry Brown/John Calipari Coaches Retreat" wasn't exactly novel. In the past, many high-profile coaches have assembled members of their coaching trees and trusted allies to swap war stories and share basketball strategies, drills, and plays.

What I think makes our annual three-day retreat special is that the event has become as much about helping one another as it is about learning Xs and Os from one another. Our profession, like so many, is about relationships and networking.

Stability in coaching is somewhat of an oxymoron. The revered, celebrated coach of 2003 can be the unemployed, degraded coach of 2005. At both the college and the NBA level it seems to be happening with more and more frequency as university budgets and franchise bottom lines seem to impact on personnel decisions more than all the other factors combined. It is, quite literally, a win-or-go-home world we live in. While the people in my profession are not expecting sympathy—especially the handsomely compensated among us—the stark reality is, every year we see friends, colleagues, and acquaintances lose their jobs suddenly and often for ludicrous reasons.

Coach Brown and I had so many people who had played for us at the college and pro levels and coached with us at various stops that our thought was, "Let's really look after one another and not just say that we do."

It's easy to make a conciliatory phone call when a peer gets let go, but it's more meaningful to actually reach out and offer that person an outlet in which he can quickly realize he is not alone and his emotions and uncertainness are not unique. Rare is the coach who goes through a career without losing at least one job.

At the 2007 retreat, former Sacramento Kings head coach Eric Musselman spoke to our group about this very topic. Eric (who was also Golden State's head coach from 2002 to 2004 and runner-up in Coach of the Year voting in 2003) was fired after just one season with the Kings in 2006–07.

"I got 211 phone calls when I was hired by the Kings," Eric said. "When I got fired, I don't think I had 11 in four months."

Stories like Eric's are all too common in our business, and everywhere really. People love a winner, but no one seems to care for the loser. It's our responsibility to reverse that and help one another.

At the retreat, we care for everyone with a connection to our "family." It started off with a couple of dozen folks, and now we have seen the numbers double. We are now inviting people who had helped our "family" of coaches or those who had fallen on tough times themselves. Employed and unemployed coaches alike from Jeff Van Gundy to Terry Porter; Tim Floyd to John Lucas; Eric Musselman to Mike Fratello; Isiah Thomas to Larry Eustachy; Tom Crean to Mike Woodson; Jay Wright to Sean Miller; Del Harris to Bob Boyd have all taken part in the clinic portion. More important, they have contributed to the confidence building and reassuring that occurs during our dinners and social times together.

Every year I marvel at the diversity of people in attendance at the gathering. We have head coaches and assistants from all levels and locations of basketball. Some are beginning their careers, others are winding down, and still others are out of the game altogether yet still remain close to men they mentored and guided through the ranks. When you take away all the glitz of the NBA arenas and all the pomp of the college campuses, what you really have is a collection of people who absolutely, to their very core, love the game of basketball and cherish the relationships and opportunities it has brought them.

Southern Mississippi Coach Larry Eustachy, who had gone through a substantial bounce back after resigning as head coach at Iowa State in 2003—which led to his admission of alcoholism—spoke at the 2007 retreat, and some of his most poignant words were, "It's not what happens to you; it's how you react to it." "I forgot where I came from even with the little success I had to that point," he said. "I thought I was going to relive my college years as a rock star at Iowa State. Knowing I have this collection of people to support me and help me through means so much to me."

That's what it's all about—looking out for one another and helping guys through the tough times and celebrating the successes and achievements. That's what families do for one another, and it's what our Coaches Retreat is based on. Our jobs are to promote one another at every opportunity. By joining together each year, we get to know more and more about one another and become better prepared to promote and advocate for everyone in our extended family.

I make it a point to reach out to peers on my "coaching family tree"—and others—when they're going through rough stretches. Sometimes I do nothing more than give my friend an opportunity to laugh for a few minutes. Other times we discuss strategy and motivational methods.

Bruiser Flint, my former assistant and the current head coach at Drexel University in Philadelphia, tells the story of one of our phone calls during the 2007–08 season.

"My Drexel team was going through a six-game losing streak and a tough season overall (we finished 12–20), and Cal calls to see how I'm doing," Bruiser recalled. "Now, remember, this was the year they went to the Final Four. He hadn't lost a game yet, and at that point they were probably like twenty games into their twenty-six-game win streak—and ranked No. 1 in the nation. First thing he says to me is, 'Bru, I know exactly what you're going through.'

"I cracked up," Bruiser said. "I was like, 'Cal, you haven't lost a game!' How do you know what I'm going through!"

But I really did know what Bruiser was experiencing. Our first couple of years at both UMass and Memphis were full of struggles for us. Even though I was on a great streak when I called Bru, you better believe I remember what it felt like to be on the other side.

At the end of each year's retreat, I make it a point to tell everyone that they need to stay in touch not just with me and not just with Coach Brown, but with everyone. We give out a list of contact information for everyone who attended.

On our family's ladder, *everyone* is looking over his shoulder to help others.

> **PractiCal Point:** Continue your bounce back even when your personal goals have been met; grow and prosper as you become the flame for others.

• • •

There are going to be some moments during your reentry and in the months and years following it where you may begin to ask yourself, like the Talking Heads once did, "Well, how did I get here?"

It will be a worthwhile question to explore and one I found myself contemplating in the days and weeks after I took the Kentucky job in April 2009. It had been a whirlwind from when my Memphis team was eliminated from the NCAA Tournament in late March to my hiring at Kentucky and eventually to our family moving full-time to Lexington. I hit the ground running and kept on running at a sprinter's pace.

When I was finally able to soak it all in and appreciate the good fortune that I, Ellen, and the kids had been blessed with, I began to think back on everything that had led me to the Bluegrass State.

I thought of all those days in my backyard hitting game-winning shots. I thought of my high school coach in Moon, Bill Sacco, who had such a profound impact on me and my college coach at Clarion, Joe DeGregorio, who also shaped my views on the game and on life. It brought back memories of working for Coach Brown at Kansas and soaking up all his lessons like a sponge. I remembered getting hired at UMass, the hours upon hours of hard work and all the good friends we made in Amherst. My Memphis recollections were also of endless hours and special people.

And, yes, I recalled back to that day when the New Jersey Nets rocked my world and the night Kansas walked off the court victorious over my Tigers. The anxiety I felt, the sense of failure, and the emotions that accompanied those downturns are never going to wash away—nor do I want them to. Neither should you.

Everything that has happened up to this point in your life is part of what makes you. The fact that you're now well into your bounce back and again in control of your life is a testament to the foundation you were able to establish during your prior years.

You've probably sensed by now that I do place a certain amount of trust in fate. Things really do happen for a reason, and no matter how unfair or devastating they may seem while you're going through them, there will be a realization down the road that everything happened for a reason.

I was reminded of this quite quickly after I started out at Kentucky. On the second Sunday of April 2009, I was catching up on some reading in my Lexington hotel room, and I had the Masters golf tournament on the television. It was one of the most riveting Sundays in Masters history as two of the game's biggest stars, Phil Mickelson and Tiger Woods, put forth a round for the ages.

But neither of those great golfers was *the* story of the 2009 Masters. Neither, for that matter, was the eventual winner, Angel Cabrera. The man I—and a nation of golf fans—became fixated on was Kentucky-native Kenny Perry. Over the span of about thirty minutes, Kenny went from the cusp of immortality to the reality of a stunning, almost incomprehensible defeat on golf's most famous stage.

With a two-shot lead and two holes to play, there would have to be a perfect storm of things going wrong to prevent Perry, forty-eight, from wearing the coveted green sport jacket that accompanies victory at Augusta. Even I—who had seen a perfect storm pass right in front of my eyes—couldn't have imagined what was about to happen to Kenny, who had won only thirteen times in more than a quarter century on the PGA Tour.

At the seventeenth he bogeyed the hole but still had a one-shot lead over his closest competitors, Chad Campbell and Cabrera. If he could make par or better on eighteen—which he'd done the three previous rounds—Kenny would become the oldest Masters champion ever and the oldest player ever to win one of golf's four majors.

"For that," Kenny later told me, "I might have gotten into the Golf Hall of Fame."

Instead, with another bogey on eighteen, Kenny wound up in a three-player playoff, eventually falling to Cabrera on the second hole of sudden death. It took a miraculous shot from Cabrera from amidst the trees to even allow him to reach the second hole against Perry (Campbell fell out after a bogey on the first hole of the playoff). Kenny Perry's perfect storm struck on golf's most hallowed grounds.

To say I could empathize with Kenny would be a major understatement. Like Kenny, I had watched the winds and seas churn as my team's dreams faded in the title game against Kansas. Come to find out, our experiences had many parallels—as most bounce backs do. Kenny, in 1996, had lost in a heartbreaking fashion to Mark Brooks (in a playoff) at the PGA Championship held in Kenny's home state at Valhalla. That, he now knows, was his first trigger event, and it prepared him for his second one at the Masters.

"It took me three years, literally, to get over that loss at Valhalla," said Kenny, now forty-nine, a member of the Kentucky Sports Hall of Fame. "But when the Masters thing happened, I had kind of been there, done that, so I was able to be more resilient."

What is most incredible to me about Kenny's tale is that the media stories in the days after his loss were not about giving up a two-shot lead in the span of two holes and losing the tournament. Instead, almost each and every writer and commentator focused on how gracious Kenny had been in defeat.

"That's just how I was raised and brought up [in Franklin, Kentucky]," Kenny said. "I believe in sportsmanship, and you know what? In the end I'm a winner. That's how I'm looking at it.

"I wanted that green jacket more than anything, but there can only be one winner, and Angel earned it. If that is the worst thing that happens to me and my family, I will have had a wonderful, wonderful life."

Kenny received thousands of letters and emails commending him on his postmatch demeanor and tact. People of all ages and from all walks of life—including former president George W. Bush and golf legend Arnold Palmer—all reached out to tell Kenny how inspiring he had been in a moment that was so obviously over-whelming.

I, too, called Kenny soon after the Masters. We talked for about thirty minutes and had an instant connection that we both acknowledged.

"It means so much to me to have you call, Coach," said Kenny, who promised to come to one of our games at Rupp Arena during the 2009–10 season. "I remember watching your game and thinking, *game over,* when you had that lead. It's a similar situation to what I went through."

Of course, Kenny was the one controlling his own destiny, and I was part of a team that required everyone to be firing on the same cylinders at the same time. But the perspective we both gained from our bounce-back experiences is almost identical. Kenny's runner-up check wasn't too shabby, and I was fine financially after the Nets canned me—but you realize by now that bounce backs are more about the mental and emotional side than the dollars and cents.

"My mom's fighting cancer, and my dad has four stents in his heart," Kenny said. "There are bigger things. What hurt me most was seeing how the Masters affected my three children [two girls and a boy, all in their early twenties]. But in the long run, they'll learn from it. It was a good teaching moment.

"I told them, 'I was going to be the same no matter what, whether I won or lost,'" Kenny said. "The 1996 thing really helped me because I wouldn't allow myself to let [the Masters] eat me up the way I did Valhalla." Nearly three months after the Masters, Kenny won the Travelers Championship in Hartford, Connecticut. It was his first win since Augusta, but his fifth in just over a year, the most of anyone on Tour during that stretch. The Hartford win also moved him into first place of the FedEx Cup standings for 2009. I bet you Kenny will tell you he never would have been able to reach the heights he has at this stage of his career without the bounce back from Valhalla. The Masters loss was tough to take for him, but it wasn't impossible to overcome.

Kenny and I have gained the knowledge you now have as a member of my bounce-back team: no matter how low you are feeling right now, no matter how dire your circumstance, there *are* better days ahead. Former U.S. senator Max Cleland from Georgia once said, "Without pain there is no pleasure, without valleys there are no mountaintops, and without struggle there is no sense of achievement."

You have achieved a great deal throughout your time on my team, and now you are a lifetime member—as long as you accept the responsibility of guiding others through turbulent times. Remember, your bounce back never ends.

> **PractiCal Point:** Understand and store the lessons you learned during this bounce back and be able to utilize your knowledge during your next one.

• • •

As a youngster growing up in Moon Township, Pennsylvania, I vividly remember listening to Kentucky basketball games with legendary announcer Caywood Ledford describing the action of Adolph Rupp's teams of the late 1960s and early 1970s. For basketball junkies of my generation—I turned fifty in February 2009—Kentucky basketball was the ultimate. There was Notre Dame football and Kentucky basketball, and everyone else was just playing catch-up.

When Kentucky athletic director Mitch Barnhart first contacted me about the Kentucky job in late March 2009, I was almost speechless—and that's saying something for me! There are certain jobs in every industry that you just can't say no to. In college basketball, Kentucky is one of those jobs.

After days of back-and-forth conversations, meetings with trusted family and confidants, I finally decided that no matter how hard it would be to leave Memphis—a city my family and I had truly grown to love—I couldn't pass up the opportunity to coach at college basketball's all-time winningest program.

Bounce backs from job loss, divorce, sickness, or any kind of setback don't follow along a neatly drawn line—they meander and wander and sometimes take years, even decades, to fully develop. Little did I know it when I began this book, but my own personal bounce back from when I was fired in 1999 by the New Jersey Nets hadn't culminated with that national title-game appearance at Memphis. Nor had it ended with all the successes we were able to achieve there over nine seasons.

No. In fact, I now know more than ever that my bounce back will never end—and neither will yours. That's the magical thing about having the strength and desire to put the past behind you and continue living your "second life" with more passion and enthusiasm than you did your "first life." I never could have imagined, after being publicly humiliated by the New Jersey Nets, that Kentucky is where I would end up a decade later. Never in my wildest dreams, but here I am.

Let that serve as a final inspiration from me to you. Even with all the remarkable experiences I have had since my firing, I am still discovering new results and offshoots of my own bounce back. As it turns out, the Memphis job was my reentry opportunity that started my bounce back moving forward; the Kentucky job will be the one that defines my bounce back.

You have endured the pain, the valleys, and the struggles. Now it's time for the achievements to take you to the mountaintops. You are stronger than you ever knew, and I'm sure of it because without my experience after being fired by the Nets, I never would have been able to go through the aftermath of the Kansas loss.

I grew and learned, and now I have been able to teach. The circle is almost complete for both of us—it's just a case of continuing to do all the courageous things you did during your bounce back and then being there for others who need help on their bounce back paths.

As I tell my players when they leave our program, know that I will always be your coach and I hope you will always be a valued member of my team. Let's share what we've been through and teach these lessons to others who need inspiration and a path.

Let's make that online community at **www.coachcalbounceback .com** as big and as powerful as possible.

Let's all bounce back, bounce forward, and bounce forever.

ACKNOWLEDGMENTS

When you've been as privileged to experience so many wonderful moments as I have, the list of people who've touched your life and helped you along the way could be a book in and of itself.

I hope all those people know how grateful and appreciative we are of their support and how special it is to have everyone share in our successes, and, yes, our bounce backs too.

For purposes of this book I have to single out all the staff members at both Memphis and Kentucky who make my life easier through their own dedication and hard work. To all my players, past and present, I thank you for the opportunities that you have helped make possible by believing in yourself, in our system, and in me. You have no idea how much it means to be called "Coach" by each and every one of you.

I had an incredibly dedicated and loyal Kitchen Cabinet that challenged me through the entire writing process, and I'd like to acknowledge them individually.

David Black is an All-Star agent and a dear friend; Dominick Anfuso went through his own inspiring bounce back during the course of this book and yet he still managed to edit and guide me through every step of the process with expertise and sincerity; Leah Miller was never more than an email away with an answer, insight, and a cheerful message; Dr. Bob Rotella kept me mentally focused and on task; Harvey Mackay's advice has been invaluable; Ken Blanchard is a long time friend and a mentor; Joe Malone always kept things positive, especially in the early days when the book's structure was lacking; Bob Marcum continued to do what he does best: tell it like it is.

To Bobbie LaPorte and Glenn Mangurian, two University of Massachusetts alumni (like my daughter Erin!), I can't thank you enough for your expertise and the amazing inspiration you provided. Lunetha Pryor, my decade-long assistant, your patience and thoroughness never go unnoticed.

And lastly, to you, a valued member of my team, thank you for allowing me to coach you through this period of your life and for becoming a member of our bounce-back family.

—John Calipari

* * *

I'm eternally grateful to Coach Calipari for having the faith in me to help convey his amazing message and become a part of his basketball family. We have both come a long way from our days in Amherst, Massachusetts, and this chance to reconnect with you has been an honor and a privilege. Bob Marcum, you made this book happen and you know what that means to Coach and me. And thanks to Shirley, Basil, Karen, Lisa, Stacey, Lou, Jake, Liza, Paul Newman, Bill Snider, Dan Wetzel, and Percy the Dog—mine is a Kitchen Cabinet filled with people (and a dog) of diverse abilities.

—David Scott

APPENDIX A

Cal's Elite 8 Meaningful Motivational Messages

Here are a few items of motivation I have used and appreciated over the years; I hope some of them will strike a chord with you:

"Good is our enemy; dare to be great."

On My Honor I Pledge to Ache.
I Will Keep My Body Powerful,
My Desire Intense, and My Will **Unflinching.**
I Will Create, by Example,
a New Definition of Passion
and I Will Continue to Cherish My Belief
that Every Inspired Drop of Sweat Is an
Investment in Perfection.

"Hard isn't hard enough for Coach Cal."
—Harper Williams, former UMass player

"We are what we repeatedly do.
Excellence, then, is not an act, but a habit."
—Aristotle

"It's easy to have faith in yourself and discipline
when you're a winner, when you're No. 1.
What you've got to have is faith and discipline
when you are not yet a winner."
—Vince Lombardi

Attitudes are contagious . . . is yours worth catching?
—Author unknown

One fails forward toward success.
An inventor fails 999 times, and if he succeeds once, he's in.
He treats his failures simply as practice shots.
—Charles F. Kettering

I know that I'm never as good or bad as any
single performance. I've never believed my critics
or my worshippers, and I've always been able to
leave the game at the arena.
—Charles Barkley

APPENDIX B

Cal's Bounce-Back Resources

On Bouncing Back

Coach Cal's Bounce Back Team website:
www.coachcalbounceback.com or **www.coachcal.com**

Career Help

Career coach: www.bobbielaporte.com

Career and behavioral attitude analysts:
www.yourhireauthority.com

Job aggregator site: www.indeed.com

Career networking sites: www.LinkedIn.com and
www.plaxo.com

Peer-to-peer community: www.imantri.com

Interviewing techniques/strategies: www.job-interview.net

On Divorce

Divorce laws, attorney references: www.aboutdivorce.com

Dealing with divorce, group support: www.divorcecare.com

On Bankruptcy/Foreclosure

Information/Resources: www.uscourts.gov/bankruptcycourts.html

Foreclosure: www.hud.gov/foreclosure

On Depression/Illness

National Institute of Mental Health: www.nimh.nih.gov/index.shtml

MentalHelp.net: www.mentalhelp.net

U.S. Department of Health and Human Service: www.hhs.gov

On Substance Abuse

National Institute on Drug Abuse: www.drugabuse.gov

Substance Abuse & Mental Health Services Administration:
www.samhsa.gov

Specific Support Groups and Help

Alcoholics Anonymous: www.aa.org

Narcotics Anonymous: www.na.org

Al-Anon: www.al-anon.alateen.org

Gamblers Anonymous: www.gamblersanonymous.org

Sexaholics Anonymous: www.sa.org

Debtors Anonymous: www.debtorsanonymous.org

Eating Disorders: www.nationaleatingdisorders.org

Anger Management (and more): www.apa.org/topics

APPENDIX C

Summary of PractiCal Points

1. Remember, your trigger event will impact on others around you, so you need to be strong for them.

2. Let the emotions run their course, and then focus on starting your bounce back with a positive attitude.

3. Speak honestly and openly about what you're going through, and accept the fact that your bounce back is in an embryonic stage.

4. Take stock of what has happened, and be prepared to attack your bounce back with passion and a positive attitude—no matter what.

5. You have to move forward and not look backward.

6. Develop a regular routine to keep you grounded and looking forward.

7. Maintain perspective, and a good sense of humor won't be far behind.

8. Trust that good things will come from where you are now.

9. Don't only recall the good, and realize there were also things that were less than ideal. From that you will appreciate the vast opportunities ahead of you.

10. Know that you are not the first, worst, or only. Others

have been where you are and they're doing just fine now. But it took some time.

11. Prepare yourself for an honest self-evaluation and serious introspection.

12. Assess your past situation objectively and honestly, and be willing to mend fences.

13. Determine what the best-version-of-yourself should look like, and show it to everybody.

14. Work to reaching a point where you are empowered by your confidence, positive attitude, and flexibility.

15. Think long and hard about what it is you want to do next and then what you want to do after that.

16. Get specific and detailed about how you will capitalize on the reentry opportunity you will receive.

17. Dream big and don't let anyone tell you that your dreams are unrealistic; they are *your* dreams and you're entitled to each and every one.

18. Realize there is nothing that is out of reach when you are part of a shared vision that serves as an inspiration to all involved.

19. Pursue your goals with the blissful determination and enthusiasm of a twelve-year-old.

20. Appreciate the unexpected outcomes your trigger event will lead to and whom you will affect.

21. Write down what you are going to discuss with your Kitchen Cabinet (or others) and prioritize that list.

22. Let your Kitchen Cabinet know you value their opinion and can't have them being afraid to speak their minds.

23. Purposely allowing frank and direct communication with those around you benefits not only your bounce

back but the overall morale and input of everyone you are leaning on.

24. Realize you've been to the mountaintop before, and you can get there again.

25. Find significance again through charitable endeavors or some type of community involvement, and make giving to others a priority in your life.

26. Make everything your own, and use each positive step forward to build your confidence for the task ahead.

27. Stay upbeat, and don't become the caller ID no one wants to see.

28. Prepare yourself to be the impulsion that drives your revitalization forward, and take pride in your ability to control your future.

29. Get feedback from people who were around you when your fall was taking place.

30. Allow others to help you, reach out to them, and don't be too proud to accept their offers.

31. Dream it, say it, talk about it, and someone will come knocking at your door.

32. Be open to every opportunity, and view everyone you meet as a potential character in your bounce-back story.

33. Rediscover your own swagger, put it forth, but don't let it become cocky arrogance.

34. Decide what you want your brand identity to be, and then own it.

35. Recognize that you have achieved incredible results in your bounce back, but that doesn't mean there won't be hitches and impediments. Fight through them with fervor.

36. Acknowledge that taking a step backward to move

forward is not the worst thing as long as you keep your ultimate goal in sight.

37. Gain a clear vision of what your reinvention might encompass and assess the reality of that vision.

38. Focus on a concrete mission objective that will serve as your bounce-back reentry point, and maintain the same vigorous and unyielding attitude you've established throughout these weeks, months, and years.

39. Research whatever the opportunity is that is in your sights, and then research and investigate some more *and* be sure to keep emotions out of your decisions and pursuits.

40. Do your homework and be prepared to capitalize on the best available opportunity.

41. Be at peace with your decision, and know you are about to embark on an unimaginable journey of joy.

42. All the energy you are putting into your bounce back now will serve you many years down the road and position you for the very best that life has to offer.

43. Take pride in where you have landed in your bounce back, but also realize the hard work is far from over.

44. Take stock of all the good and bad parts of your first life and keep only the best aspects as you begin your second life.

45. Make yourself indispensable by doing the dirty work, and watch the doors it opens for you in your bounce back. Be as positive and as motivational as you can—leave an impression on everyone you encounter.

46. Look under the rug, but don't start sweeping until you have had time to get input from those who have institutional knowledge of the situation.

47. Be prepared for early setbacks, and use those experiences to bolster every aspect of your bounce back.

48. Notice the lessons you are learning during every step of your bounce back; take the time to process and understand these lessons.

49. Allow the crises of the past and interruptions in your progress to become unifying events and personal growth opportunities.

50. Tinker and experiment to bring about incredible results—just be sure to proceed with caution.

51. Get by the anxiety, get by the fear, and then there is courage. You can't be afraid to make a mistake—I tell my players, "Just go play."

52. Continue your bounce back even when your personal goals have been met; grow and prosper as you become the flame for others.

53. Understand and store the lessons you learned during this bounce back and be able to utilize your knowledge during your next one.

APPENDIX D

John Calipari's Head-Coaching Record

Season	Team	W-L	Pct.	Accomplishments
1988–89	UMass	10–18	.357	
1989–90	UMass	17–14	.548	NIT
1990–91	UMass	20–13	.606	NIT Final Four
1991–92	UMass	30–5	.857	A-10 Champ (R/T); NCAA Sweet 16
1992–93	UMass	24–7	.774	A-10 Champ (R/T); NCAA 2nd Rd.
1993–94	UMass	28–7	.800	A-10 Champ (R/T); NCAA 2nd Rd.
1994–95	UMass	29–5	.853	A-10 Champ (R/T); NCAA Elite 8
1995–96	UMass	35–2	.946	A-10 Champ (R/T); NCAA Final Four
1996–97	NJ Nets	26–56	.317	
1997–98	NJ Nets	43–39	.524	NBA Playoffs
1998–99	NJ Nets	3–17	.150	
2000–01	Memphis	21–15	.583	NIT Final Four
2001–02	Memphis	27–9	.750	C-USA Div. Champ; NIT Champ
2002–03	Memphis	23–7	.767	C-USA Nat'l Div. Champ; NCAA
2003–04	Memphis	22–8	.733	C-USA Champ (R); NCAA 2nd Rd.
2004–05	Memphis	22–16	.579	NIT Final Four
2005–06	Memphis	33–4	.892	C-USA Champ (R/T); NCAA Elite 8
2006–07	Memphis	33–4	.892	C-USA Champ (R/T); NCAA Elite 8
2007–08	Memphis	38–2	.950	C-USA Champ (R/T); NCAA Title Game
2008–09	Memphis	33–4	.892	C-USA Champ (R/T); NCAA Sweet 16
NCAA Totals		**445–140**	**.761**	

Two-time Naismith Men's College Coach of the Year (1996, 2008)

Sports Illustrated National Coach of the Year, 2009

ABOUT THE AUTHORS

John Calipari is the current head coach of the University of Kentucky men's basketball program and a veteran of nearly twenty college seasons at the University of Memphis and the University of Massachusetts. Widely regarded as one of the greatest program builders in all of college basketball, Calipari has led his teams to earn ten conference titles, eleven NCAA Tournament berths, and two Final Fours. He received the national Naismith Men's College Coach of the Year Award for both the 1995–96 and 2007–08 seasons, as well as the *Sports Illustrated* National Coach of the Year honor for 2008–09. A highly sought-after motivational speaker, Calipari and his wife, Ellen, have three children, Erin, Megan, and Bradley.

* * *

David Scott is the former senior writer and editor at *SPORT* magazine. His work has appeared in *Sports Illustrated for Kids, The Boston Globe Magazine, Men's Fitness,* and *FHM.* In 2000, Scott was recognized by *The Best American Sports Writing* for "One in a Million: The Tim Bishop Story." Scott first worked with Coach Calipari while an undergraduate at the University of Massachusetts. He lives in Hull, Massachusetts.